Three Women in a Boat

Three Women in a Boat

Kim Taplin

Drawings by Emma Whiting

i
impact books

First published in Great Britain 1993 by
Impact Books, 112 Bolingbroke Grove, London SW11 1DA

ISBN 1 874687 13 7

Typeset by Roger King Graphic Studios, Poole, Dorset.
Printed and bound by The Guernsey Press, Guernsey.

To my mother and father

1

My original copy of *Three Men in a Boat* got lost
somewhere between the ante-natal and the labour ward.

We had a cat we called Bibby at the time, of hidden
origins but with an aristocratic, Persian look. A romantic
foundling, it had appeared one day, mewing and wild, from
under the floorboards of the library where I worked, and
had savaged the librarian who offered it milk. Next day I
came equipped with some thick gloves and took it home,
where it grew into a fine hunting blue-grey tom with
omniverous tastes and very bad breath. He stayed until we
lent the house out while we were away on holiday, mainly
so that he could go on living in the manner to which he was
accustomed. Unfortunately, the visitors had a cat too, a
burly brute they called Stripomenos, and whether Bibby
(whose full name was Biblion) challenged him to combat
and was slain and they didn't like to tell us, or whether he
merely felt his noble soul could not co-exist with this
plebeian rival and so left to pursue his quest, we never saw
him again. We often fancied we saw him, straying, grey,
and seen by rare glimpses, like the Scholar Gipsy; but the
vision always vanished before we could get to it, or turned
out to be some other cat.

But at the time, as I say, Bibby lived beneath a roof, our
roof, and had that morning introduced a mole under it as

well. A mole was a new departure. He'd brought in shrews, mice, voles, birds, rats and rabbits before, but not a mole. It was a self-effacing guest, and we had an exciting time catching up with it and finally trapping it under an upturned pudding-basin as it tried to tunnel under the staircarpet. By this time the contractions that had woken me up in the small hours were distinctly closer together, and I thought I might venture to present myself at the hospital as a pretty serious candidate for maternity.

It was in the days of big wards, and a dozen or so women lay round the room in attitudes of restful dejection. Some of them listlessly turned the pages of magazines featuring discouragingly smiling and beautiful mothers holding unnaturally serene and unblemished babies. One or two were knitting the ritual garments that most self-respecting infants are at no time actually small enough to wear, or which if they are they will rapidly learn to kick off or cover with indelible blackcurrant, or egg yolk, or vomit. Most merely lay and gazed out at the world over their swollen bellies in a kind of torpor.

I smiled round nervously, and then clutched hold of the side of the bed and lost touch. Returning to my social self, I tried to appear unruffled. Stoicism was clearly the order of the day. No-one was to reveal, by the least twitch of a muscle, that anything was happening at all, let alone these shattering intimations of new life. For this my reading offered an explanation. I remembered how in Flora Thompson's *Lark Rise to Candleford* that after the grimmest of unanaesthetised deliveries the Oxfordshire women of a hundred years ago would murmur, 'I didn't flinch, did I? Oh, I do hope I didn't flinch'. It seemed the local mores were still in force.

They were astonishing, these women. Early Christian martyrs the lions had had a first snap at were simply nowhere. I did my best not to grunt or make faces. They seemed so calm and dignified, I felt it would have been to commit a terrible social gaffe, really letting the side down. I tried not to catch their eyes. I would look at them covertly between pangs, and the more I looked the more I was impressed by their extraordinary sang-froid. British spies undergoing interrogation, or members of the Foreign Legion lining up for field amputation, wouldn't have had a touch on them. It was unnerving. They seemed to be made in a different mould from mine. Did they have some secret, some technique I wasn't privy to?

A woman in the corner bed wearing an extraordinary confection in pink nylon looked particularly peaceful, and as I took in its gentle rise and fall with envy and admiration it dawned on me that she was actually asleep. This was too much. Probably it was far too late for me to be initiated, but I had to know what was going on. I felt I took a risk in revealing my ignorance, but my curiosity won. As soon as the next spasm was safely past, I seized the moment, and turning to the next bed with a propitiatory smile, hoping its occupant had been as absorbed in her reading as she appeared, I asked hesitantly:

'Is *everyone* in this ward in labour?'

At the word she laid down her magazine and stared at me as though I had an infectious illness. Then she turned to the bed on the other side and murmured urgently.

'She's *what?*' asked the other side incredulously.

At this point I was once more overtaken by something wringing me out quite fiercely, and when it had finished, and shaken me and hung me on the line, I found that everyone in the room was looking at me, including the woman in pink, who must have been woken up for the purpose.

'Nur-urse! Nur-urse!' called the woman nearest to the door on a note of alarm.

It gradually began to dawn on me that far from being the new girl who didn't know the ropes and wasn't coming up to scratch, I was the heroine of the hour, captain of hockey, the one who pioneered. What I was undergoing was what they were all waiting for. Trying once more to rise to the occasion I did my best to assume an expression of calm superiority, mingled with a touch of the deep and slightly sad expression about the eyes that comes from having lived and suffered.

Nurse seemed put out when she came, as though I had deliberately misled the authorities in some way. But she acted fast. She went away and before the next contraction she was back with a colleague and a trolley, onto which they briskly loaded me and my possessions, for all the world like a couple of the station porters you could still see occasionally in those days. This deflated me a bit. It is hard to look noble when you are being treated like a piece of luggage. And it was at this point that one of my effects, the comforting, familiar book I had brought to cheer me through, must have been mislaid.

Soon I was on another floor in a ward with cubicles, where I and others lay fermenting in the way ordained for us. Had we been able to see each other I think we should have felt more mutual sympathy. As it was there was the pretence of privacy without the peace, and I assume the others felt as irritated by my presence as I did by theirs. On one side a woman was urging the nurses to 'Tell my 'usband what I'm goin' through, and make 'im say we'll never 'ave any more', while on the other a Pakistani woman was crying 'Aieee! Aieee!' loudly and incessantly, to the obvious relief and satisfaction of her feelings, and oblivious of the contempt of the English nurses. I must have made some kind of noise myself, because I remember a rather sharp-faced girl with green fingernails telling me to 'pull myself together'. So I suppose it is not without significance that it was upon entering this adult, and very female, world that I lost that insouciant masterpiece of knicker-wettingly facetious humour which had so lighted up my youth. I hadn't exactly elected to put away childish things but they had somehow been taken from me all the same ...

2

It was my mother who had first introduced me to *Three Men in a Boat*, as she did also to the delight of rowing. Taking the train to Maidenhead and going out for a day on the river was one of the high spots of my childhood, as the hours spent in or about the River Itchen were among the happiest times of hers. I am persuaded that there are few joys so great, few things we can set against the minus so effective as communicating an enthusiasm. I also read *The Wind in the Willows* at about the same time, and began what may well have been my own first book, of which I can remember little beyond the title, *Up River Tales,* and the fact that one of the characters was a moorhen.

It was not until many years later that I saw the old black and white film called *The Passing of the Third Floor Back*, based on a play by Jerome K. Jerome. It is a whimsical, innocent and serious piece, in which God takes a room in a lodging-house for a while – and incidentally treats his fellow lodgers to a curative river trip; and although it is quite different in form and manner from *Three Men in a Boat*, it made me realise that one reason I had responded so strongly to Jerome was that touch of the mystic in his make-up. I saw that the purple passages and the philosophical hints in *Three Men in a Boat* were seriously meant, despite the fact that his sense of the absurd and his nose for pomposity would always so healthily move in to subvert his moralising self. And that it's a consequence of his wonderful ability to laugh at himself, which he does in the persona of J., that the job of keeping us readers earthed is always given to Harris or George.

So when I came recently upon Jerome's autobiography *My Life and Times* I was at first utterly astonished to read what he said of *Three Men in a Boat,* but I soon, on reflection, could believe it:

> I did not intend to write a funny book, at first. I did not know I was a humourist. I never have been sure about it. In the middle ages, I should probably have gone about preaching and got myself burnt or hanged.

I was more surprised, though I suppose in the light of the classic personality of the sad clown I should not have been, to find him speaking of his 'melancholy, brooding disposition'. In fact I was so familiar with his gentle irony in revealing the vanities of J's character that I was at first inclined to laugh, as though Humpty Dumpty had described himself as having a slender, sylph-like physique. But then he went on to say that he had acquired this bent from living amidst the poverty of London's East End as a young child, and I realised he was serious. And he concludes by saying, 'Look where I will, there seems to me always more sadness than joy in life.'

Seen as the product of a temperament that experienced life in this way, my liking for the man and his book if possible increased. In another book he called *Novel Notes* Jerome quotes or invents the words of a nurse to whom he has suggested she write about the insights into human

suffering she has had in the course of her profession. She
replies:

> If you'd seen as much sorrow in the world as I have, you
> wouldn't want to write a sad book ... I think it can only be
> the people who have never *known* suffering who can care to
> read of it. If I could write a book, I should like to write a
> merry book – a book that would make people laugh.

The fact that a nurse is speaking highlights the connection
between healing and writing. Of course it isn't simple. To
begin with, books don't divide straightforwardly into sad
and merry ones; and in any case I take the remark rather as
Jerome's assertion of the status of comedy, of its at least
equal value to the world, rather than as a denigration of
tragedy. But if there is one article of a creative credo that I
have never yet doubted, it is that merry or sad we should
be in business to heal – though it can work in a thousand
different ways.

I am not advocating nothing but happy endings, nor
moralising, nor sentiment, nor over-simplification, nor
closure. I am speaking of an encounter between writer and
reader from which the reader emerges feeling better, even
though he may have been harrowed. Creative writing is
something that we give; I see a book as a present. Even the
recounting of very terrible facts can heal provided that
healing, however radical the necessary surgery, is the
intention behind the telling. If there is no intention beyond
making us share the revealed pain then the writer differs
little from the torturer whose practices he describes.
Likewise if the laughter is at someone else's pain. There
are times for simply showing the raw wound – in
journalism, in therapy or with our friends, in the

confessional. But I believe that art does something more.

And of course it's a two-way thing. The reader has to be ready for the gift. Looking back I can see that I have often found art's medicine too strong; and that it's perilously easy to react by saying that something is too depressing or too trivial, when trying to justify ourselves for not being strong enough to take it.

In the face of suffering Jerome's nurse wanted to write 'a merry book', and Jerome's *Three Men in a Boat* is the merriest book I know. The word 'merry' has had an interesting history. The Oxford Dictionary's definitions make very cheerful reading in themselves:

> Of things: Pleasing, agreeable ... Of a saying, jest, etc. :
> Amusing, diverting ... Of looks or appearance: Agreeable,
> bright ... Of persons, etc. : Full of animated enjoyment;
> mirthful, hilarious. Also of disposition: Given to mirth ... Of
> times or seasons: Characterized by festivity.

The word is somewhat archaic now, and when coupled with England' it probably always harked back. Robin Hood's men were merry too: there are connotations of freedom and gentle anarchy there, and a strong and healthy mockery of unjust authority rather than a bitter and impotent resentment of it. Shakespeare used it constantly. He knew that 'a merry heart goes on all day' (and uses footpaths), and that the simple outdoor life is a good one, where you 'tune your merry note unto the sweet bird's throat'.

For some reason my daughter and son and their friends took up the word, as children will sometimes a word or a catchphrase, and used it a hundred times a day. They would use it of every scheme, menu, event, outfit etc. of which they approved, but at the same time they would use it with an affectionately scornful intonation of every such scheme, menu etc. proposed by their mothers – their worldly-wise understanding seeing how innocent and mockable were our notions. Superiority thus honourably demonstrated, they could enjoy our merry schemes with a childlike zest.

Merriness is linked with innocence. I suspect this is what Jesus was getting at when he said one of his fiercer pieces about it being better to have millstones tied to you and be drowned than to offend one of the little ones who believed in him. Children don't understand theology; but children who are loved will be loving, they are natural exponents of the gospel of love, and those who darken infant lives and take away their innocence can set the minus operating from generation to generation. I don't believe Jesus believed in original sin. I think God originally believed we might choose to be merry, but must be getting a bit more doubtful about it by now. In fact God must have as much trouble believing in us as we do believing in God.

Consider also a merry-andrew, a merry-go-round, and merrymaking. And a merry-bout. This last is archaic slang for the act of love-making, and seems to carry pleasant connotations of the effect of the act upon the spirit when the spirit of the act is mutually joyful.

There are people who don't see the point of *Three Men in a Boat*, those who are too solemn, or too grown-up, or too sad. Such people see nothing but racism in *The Merchant of Venice* and nothing but snobbishness in P.G. Wodehouse. And alas, I can't even say to them 'rest you merry' as it was sometimes used with the meaning, 'I'll leave you to your opinions and not trouble you', for merry they are not. I wish them well.

Although he was coy about the fact in one of his prefaces, saying only that he was feeling 'absurdly pleased' with himself 'for reasons that concern only myself', Jerome reveals in his autobiography that he wrote *Three Men in a Boat* when he had just come back from his honeymoon 'and had the feeling that all the world's troubles were over'. It seems to me very significant that it was just at that particular time in his life that this cordial book was conceived and brought forth. Loving sex and good laughter go hand in hand. Jerome speaks rather sombrely about sex and its problems, referring to the years between puberty and marriage as 'a fearful thing'. 'I would that all men of good-feeling treated this deep mystery of our nature with more reverence. I think it would help,' he says with unusual seriousness. He was particularly distressed by the degrading attitude of his fellow males, even those he liked or admired in other ways. His word 'mystery' goes deeper than a mere dislike of smut. It affirms something.

A hundred years later contraception and changing social attitudes may have given some physiological and psychological relief, but I suspect that our spiritual well-being, our deep sex-happiness, depends on something that doesn't change at all.

Jerome wrote his book straight after his honeymoon, and I am writing mine, as it falls out, in precisely the opposite situation, at the ending of a love affair, as hurting as he was happy. He was pleased with himself; I am struggling with self-disgust. Jerome also confessed, by the way, that there was in fact no real dog. I did have a dog of sorts, one that I was particularly anxious to leave behind or to lose – the black dog of depression.

My book is partly a tribute to Jerome, whose genial spirit has befriended mine in such a clear way as to make me often declare, at least half-seriously, that I would rather have written *Three Men in a Boat* than *King Lear*. 'God be with his soul!' Juliet's Nurse said of her dead husband, ''a was a merry man', and so say I of Jerome.

Good laughter, laughter that is not bitter, like good sex, is very good for us, it is cordial. The closest Jerome comes to *schadenfreude* is showing us how we laugh when the other fellow's shirt falls in the water. My book is not in emulation of his; I have simply taken the liberty of using it – so firm and friendly a thing as it is – as my jetty, something to push off from. There are times when our lives are shadowed and the sunlight seems to mock, and we have to be weaned back on to it by degrees. Mine is a book with shadows. It is about a short journey that – as journeys do – reflects that larger one. It was written, and the journey made, in search of healing. And it is partly made up of reflections – which is something rivers are rich in.

3

Grief, spleen, need for independence, need for female
solidarity, need for a change, need to turn to tried
restoratives – all these made urgent the turning of an idea
I'd had whimsically for years into a reality. I and two
female friends would spend a week rowing up the Thames.
I thought I would take the advice that was given to
Shakespeare's Merchant of Venice:

> Seeing too much sadness hath congealed your blood,
> And melancholy is the nurse of frenzy,
> Frame your mind the mirth and merriment,
> Which bars a thousand cares and lengthens life.

One of my companions was to be an old friend who was
also licking her wounds over a man. We began to make
plans. We spent a good deal of time going through our
other female friends and deciding who was up to the mark
to go with us and who wasn't. Oh, but we were choosy, for
our third companion! One was rejected as being too frail,
another too unreliable, a third too bossy, and so on, until
we ran out of friends. It was extraordinarily reminiscent of
J., Harris and George rejecting one inn because it didn't
have honeysuckle round the door, and another because they
didn't like the boots of the man who was standing outside,
and almost ending up with nowhere to sleep. We finally

settled on a favoured one to ask: it was a huge compliment.

It turned out of course that she had several plans for her summer holiday already, and she somehow implied that even if she hadn't she would quickly have developed some. The next we approached couldn't cope with the idea of rowing, didn't think we could be serious. And so on. Then my one definite companion broke her wrist, and not only couldn't row, but couldn't do a lot of more necessary things, and so for a while I gave up the idea altogether.

Then Phoebe volunteered. The baby whose birth was impending in the first chapter, was now a strong and cheerful young woman of twenty-two. I fought off letting the idea that I was being taken pity on prevent me from accepting the offer of her company gratefully. What if I were? I could do with people being nice to me. And perhaps she would enjoy it all the same. Poor Jerome confesses in his autobiography that he was very lonely after his mother's death but turned down more than one invitation for Christmas because 'into one I had read patronage and into another compassion'. Was he in deeper grief, or did he have something pious writers used to call Proper Pride, which I'm deficient in? Or do we simply differ in temperament? He was considerably younger than me at the time, and perhaps some need to know that he could face the world alone was making itself felt. I know I can do that but don't care to, if I don't have to. I'd rather now be comfortable than proud. Which may sound odd in view of the trip I was proposing; but I mean comfortable inside.

And Phoebe's friend Emma would make the third. It seemed astonishing that a young woman of twenty-two who did not have filial sympathy to induce her would actually think it agreeable to spend a week in a small boat and a tent with her friend and her *mother*. But it is a very pleasant facet of Emma's character that she is not ageist, and has always treated me as an equal. Besides which I suppose there is an unregenerate touch of the child in mine. Whatever the reason, I get on well with her, and moreover though not what I had planned, the prospect of having the company of two women who were *not* upset over the defection of their lovers, or the menopause, or what they have failed to make of their lives, seemed suddenly an unexpected blessing. They were still young and foolish enough to think that the trip promised enjoyment. 'It'll be fun,' they said. 'It'll be a laugh.' It did me good just to hear them.

Emma's other friends were not encouraging. Reports began to filter back. One said we would not be allowed through the locks, and would have to carry the boat round. A second said that without being in strict training we hadn't a chance of lasting the week. She said if we must go it was essential that we wear gloves, but she advised against the whole enterprise. She had once rowed in a women's eight and knew about these things. Then Emma herself suddenly confessed that she couldn't row. I said 'Rubbish!' as confidently as I could to the first two objections, and 'Never mind, we'll soon teach her,' to the third, but my fragile edifice of hope immediately felt crushed.

I began to get anxious as well as depressed, a state that always makes me defer preparation and planning in a highly counter-productive and circular fashion. I managed to go and book the boat, but that was all. Actually, I think that had more than a little to do with the anxiety. The woman who hired it to me was full of good advice and experienced-sounding caveats.

'Never leave it,' she said. 'One of you must always stay with it. The boats get taken even from here, right by the house. Oh no, it's not insured. It would cost far too much to insure. If it's stolen, you are responsible. You'll need a good strong chain and padlock.'

She confided that she was very recently widowed, which helped to explain her gloomy tone. She was pessimistic about our personal safety too.

'If I were you,' she continued, while my spirits plummetted, 'I'd moor on the opposite side to the towpath. You're less likely to be interfered with. You'll have a lovely holiday,' she added hastily, seeing my expression, and obviously thinking that ninety pounds was too high a price for honesty.

I hadn't thought, when I planned the expedition, of boat thieves, or rape, or murderous attacks to make off with twenty-one pairs of knickers and a camping gaz stove. I'd thought of tranquility and freedom from care and being in the bosom of nature. And now I was going to have to be vigilant, and worry, and even perhaps in some sense be responsible for the two young people I'd thoughtlessly involved in this crazy adventure.

My daughter has a more resilient disposition than mine. I have seen her curled up in a heap, sniffing and blotchy, and within a few hours transform herself into an impressive job candidate, go in and win. I have seen her in apparent despair after failing her driving test, and five minutes later heard her joking about it on the phone to a friend. Such are the enormous blessings of an extrovert personality. In this case she didn't allow herself to be infected by my anxiety or put off by my apparent loss of interest. She got a pen and paper and made me think about what we needed to take.

This in itself was something I'd been worrying about. When I asked to see the boat the owner had waved from a distance and said, 'One of those blue ones'. Not having learned assertiveness when young, I've never quite got the hang of it. I'd felt I was being a nuisance, and needlessly importunate when I'd asked in the first place to see it – quite a reasonable request when I come to think of it. But to have asked to see it properly, and be told how to stow our things, and how to moor it, and so on, was more than I could manage.

'Oh, thanks,' I said weakly, peering anxiously, from afar.

When I thought about it afterwards, I couldn't for the life of me see how everything would fit in, since a minimum must be three of us, three rucksacks, a tent, a water container, cooking gear and food. And there wasn't even a cover.

A week or so later I was passing the place with a friend, one of those I had originally wondered about as our number three, though I hadn't ever got round to asking her. Now I told her about the proposed trip and airily pointed out the boat.

'One of those *blue* ones?!' she said, and gave me a look that I was to see again on the face of Emma's boyfriend when he came to see her off – incredulity mixed with something that all but questioned my sanity.

But she provided some practical help. I was just about to buy a tent when I saw her, and was feeling despondent about the outlay, especially as I loathe camping and didn't suppose I would ever do it again. Actually I thought I'd camped my last already years before, but now fate seemed to be decreeing otherwise. Originally I'd thought we'd stay at pubs or Bed and Breakfasts along the way, picturing the evening saunter round the pretty village and anticipating the hot bath that would relax our pleasantly tired muscles, to say nothing of the large breakfasts cooked by someone else that would set us up for the day's work. Even J. and Harris and George had done that occasionally. But a century on from then the Thames was apparently a less law-abiding river. We couldn't leave the boat. I couldn't risk having to buy a new boat: I suspected it would cost a good deal more than a tent. 'I've got a tent you can borrow,' my friend said. 'Walk along to the car with me, and you can have it now. It's in the boot as it happens.'

She happened, at just the right moment, to have a three-person tent we could have. Moreover it was one that was so modern and so easy to put up that Phoebe got the hang of it even though the instruction booklet was irreparably stuck together, and even I got the hang of it after a course of instruction from Phoebe. It was one of those timely chances that make you feel you have been watched over, or have been chatting to an angel unawares. It gave an infinitesimal upturn to my spirits, and I began to think perhaps I was meant to be doing this after all, and the universe was not against it. (By the way, it's no use writing to ask me about the tent: it is a kind only obtainable in the New World – my friend is American.) That's the truth, but it's a curious thing how life goes allegorical on you when you start on a journey.

4

We started from Folly Bridge, and to my state of mind at the time that had a definitely allegorical ring. It was also where J. and his friends turned round. I say, we started, but when I turned up neither of the others had come. It was eleven o'clock on Saturday the third of August and I asked for the boat as arranged, and the mistress of the boats said:

'What boat? We don't do boats for camping.'

Fighting my all-too-immediate sense of defeat, I reminded her of our conversation, and she then said, 'Oh, yes, that boat. I thought you meant a camping boat,' and directed me on to her son. I mouthed my request at him and he obligingly turned down his ghetto blaster and drew up number 5 for me, and put in a couple of waterproof cushions.

In the light of my latest exchange with the boat lady, and on seeing the boat at close quarters, I was beginning to wonder whether we'd somehow been at cross purposes, and I'd paid £90 to hire it for the day, rather than for the week. Or whether it was envisaged as the tender to a launch, with which I was supposedly already equipped. I was well beyond trying to be cool.

'I'm wondering how our stuff will fit in,' I said in a tone of panicky appeal. What I thought he could do about it if it didn't, I don't know. But despite his daunting post-punk appearance he had a kind soul, like my doctor, and could see what I wanted – reassurance. He hadn't even seen what 'the stuff' consisted of yet, but he said calmly:

'Oh, there's plenty of room. It's surprising how much you can put behind the seat.'

And so it proved.

It was a nicely-shaped single-sculling skiff, dark blue fibreglass inside and wood outside. It had a rudder, and shaped oars that could be removed from the rowlocks – something that later proved to be essential. I mention these things because we later came to appreciate their importance, as we learned to appraise other by-the-hour boats – which was what this usually was – with a professional eye. Seeing the clumsy tubs that were sometimes offered, with their crude, paddle-like oars, closed rowlocks and lack of rudder, we realised that to row upwards of eighty miles in one of those might have been just possible, but would have been an utterly laborious and joyless undertaking. Just then however the boat looked very small, very open, and very low in the water. J. had referred sentimentally to their 'frail little craft' – a hulking great double-sculling thing with hoops, about twice the size of this. But then this was not yet loaded up, and as I looked at it my heart, in anticipation of its certain fate, sank.

Emma now turned up, which cheered me a little once more, although her boyfriend didn't.

'See you next week,' said Emma, hugging him.

'See you tomorrow,' he replied laconically, and went. There was still no sign of Phoebe, but seeing that she'd spent the previous night at a party in London we were not altogether surprised.

The closest I could bring the car was a street on the other

side of the river that ended in some steps that came down to the water. This meant rowing across to begin with, to load up – and also back as it turned out, since there were two winos on the steps and I couldn't leave Emma there alone while I took the car some distance away to where it was to be parked for the week. The received wisdom about drunks is that they don't present a threat because they are unsteady, and if the worst comes to the worst you can push them over. But you feel pretty unsteady yourself, in a boat, especially with your potential assailants standing above you, on firm ground. Moreover these were rather younger and haler-looking than the usual winos, and it was still fairly early in the day.

'You wants ter watch out fer your daugh'er,' says one of them laboriously. 'Cause I'm the sort of bloke what's goin' to take 'er away from you. Your Mum looks cross,' he added judicially to Emma, as I reddened with annoyance and frustration.

Our gear was encased in black plastic dustbin bags in case it rained, a practical but somewhat dismal touch that made us feel an irrational distaste for the contents. But to compensate it went in beautifully, which then made us feel rather pleased with ourselves for travelling so light.

At this point Phoebe arrived, very cheerful and apologetic and, surprisingly, not the worse for wear as far as could be seen. I greeted her by getting the deep freeze off my chest.

Before leaving home she'd turned off the deep freeze what I'd worked out must have been two days ago, in mistake for the washing machine, and I'd only discovered it, by noticing a pool of water, just before leaving. I threw out the ice cream, brought the soggy fish fingers with me, told myself the rest of the stuff was still hard really, and switched the thing back on. I don't suppose the mothers in those baby magazines ever get in that sort of mess, but then they probably stay at home to check on the deep freeze all the time, and do everyone's washing for them, so it wouldn't ever get switched off by mistake, and don't have merry daughters who'll go off camping with them even when they're grown up.

Absurdly, my first instinct on starting was to grope for my seat belt. Not that sitting in a rowing boat is in the least like sitting in a car, thank goodness, but sitting down and being moved along must have pressed some button in the computer of my brain which said, *This isn't safe, you're not fastened in.* They are very queer, these phantom physical habits. Almost two years after my husband left me, and I had left off wearing my ring, some marital-seeming neurosis made me make as if to fiddle with it as I used to do when the set-up made me tense.

We were so much closer to the water than I had remembered rowing boats are. Perhaps it makes all the difference if you think you are only in them for an hour. But if we were close to the water, we were also close to nature, and almost immediately the process of converting vulnerability, nakedness, from an unwelcome and shivery and unnatural-seeming state to a welcome and free and delightful one began to take place. A coot on its open nest of rushes is king of the castle, and so are we. There is a pungent and invigorating scent from the buddleias that root themselves in any old dusty crack. I developed an affection for this plant during my suburban childhood, for the way it would cheerfully make blossom the desert of derelict sites, reminding me that there was earth underneath the thickest concrete, a sign of life, an affirmation that nature was unvanquished, and a promise that out there in 'the country', that for some reason my soul always longed for though I had never lived in it, there was still some of it left. Now it carried a whiff of nostalgia for me too, not for the pavement world of the places where I grew up, but for innocence and childishness, for a slightly less wounded self in a slightly less wounded world.

We pass by the allotments – those various and likeable tenancies of the earth, and enjoy the *jeux d'esprits* of some of the brightly painted and decorated huts on them. Both huts and choice of plants show people's individuality and affirmations. Sunflowers and roses, beans and cabbages, are mixed in a cheerful democracy. We passed a houseboat covered in tubs of flowers, house and garden in one, another witness to how abundance and beauty can co-exist with simplicity.

Several people walking on the bank look at us smilingly as if to say '*That* looks nice', perhaps responding to our awakened and purposeful expressions. Who gave who what? I reflect on the contagion of moods, even between strangers, and also how boredom is an insidious ingredient in depression, and how difficult I found the effort of getting this little expedition organised, yet how cleansed I was already beginning to feel by the opening to new experience.

Very soon the banter begins.

'That looks 'ard work,' calls a fisherman.

'Where's the man with the drum?' asks another.

It is good-humoured but it is curious. Men in a rowing-boat would not call it forth. A hundred years ago, perhaps we should have been a spectacle worth comment. J. has some fun at the expense of being towed by 'girls' or of rowing them and splashing their costumes. (I can't see how they managed it incidentally. We scarcely got splashed the whole week. But then perhaps we weren't trying to show off our speed to anyone.)

According to Jerome's autobiography, at about the time that he wrote *Three Men in a Boat*:

> *The Times* had a leader warning the nation of the danger, should woman cease to recognise that the true sphere of her development lay in the home circle. Hardly a year later, female suffrage for unmarried women householders in their own right was mooted in the House of Commons, and London rocked with laughter ... The right of a married woman to go shopping by herself, provided she got back in time for tea, had long been recognised.

Jerome himself makes out to have been reasonably sympathetic to woman's cause, although of course as many of us have come to recognise through bitter experience, it is the proclaimed feminist who is often the worst news in a personal relationship. He reminisces about how he and a co-playwright got into trouble for having a fast heroine who rode a bicycle. And he adds, sympathetically but with the jocularity that he can afford whose withers are unwrung:

> It was unwomanly, then, to ride a bicycle. There were so many things, in those days, that were unwomanly to do. It must have been quite difficult to be a woman, and remain so day after day.

We had our first lunch, at which I triumphantly made tea on the new camping gaz stove, which I had bought and assembled myself, following the instructions, although I had always been scared and incompetent over that kind of thing before, and left it to husband or son. I sat back savouring the comfort of the tea and beginning to enjoy that holiday sense of having got away and left the problems of everyday life behind for a while and entered a special space.

Phoebe complained the tea tasted of plastic, but we told her she was going to have to get used to it. We'd brought a red, a blue and a green mug; and before long we all learned to associate them with feelings of gratitude and comfort, and quite forgot what proper tea tasted like.

'You're a long way from home - boat's home anyway,' says someone, and we feel like intrepid travellers, till he adds, 'why 'aven't you got a camping skiff?' and we feel rather foolish, and vulnerable, and ill-equipped. I had tried to find somewhere to hire a boat with a cover that you put up over hoops, such as Jerome describes, but without success. This was probably just as well, because he makes them sound pretty diabolical to put up, and the whole boat would have had to be a heavier construction – the only two we passed both were – and we would almost certainly not have been able to make the journey we did in it.

5

Besides the huge flock of all but domesticated greylag geese that always live gregariously by Port Meadow among their littered feathers, that day there was a rather tame heron. It would fly a short way off and settle again, seeming weary of people but scarcely wary any more, like a creature in a zoo.

I've noticed that mallard and even moorhens seem quite to change their nature according to whether they live near human beings or not. The mallard and moorhens on the fairly sequestered stretch of the Cherwell where I live are distinctly shy. It hadn't occurred to me that the same adaptability might occur in herons, and I felt obscurely troubled by it, and then troubled that I should have been troubled. Was there some lawless part of me that opposed the coming about of the Peaceable Kingdom, that preferred the red in tooth and claw and territorialism and life-and-death alertness and sense of self? Or was there, almost worse, an element in me of that attitude so many men seem to have to women, they are eager only so long as the matter is difficult, and when what they sought is there before their eyes morning, noon and night they lose interest? Well, we can accuse ourselves of all kinds of things, and there will probably be yet worse motives in the mix that we can't reach at all. And I think it is for *this* reason that I have a deep instinct desiring the creatures to maintain their aloofness: human beings are not yet to be trusted, because we do not yet know, or perhaps have forgotten, what we are.

As a nation we British are more interested in nature than most, as anyone who has tried to buy a simple guide to the flora and fauna when abroad, or asked local people the names of things will have realised. I remember trying to buy a bird book in Greece, and all I could find was an antiquated thing by some English classical scholar on the birds in Aeschylus or Homer or some such. But even those of us who think of ourselves as nature-lovers are all to a greater or lesser extent over the ears in a lifestyle that is hostile to nature, one that pollutes earth, air and water, that performs experiments upon animals, that assumes the right to use the planet 'and all that therein is' for the short-term benefit of a rather small number of our own species. And even if we are thoroughly aware of all that, and do our best to limit the extent of our personal damage, it is impossible to opt out altogether. And so like unwilling carriers of a disease, we too aren't fit to be trusted and fraternised with.

After lunch the entire food supply seemed seriously depleted. I'd been so afraid of sinking the boat that I hadn't packed very much. Phoebe was pleased about this. She said she preferred to be flexible. By this she seemed to mean she thought there would be lots of places along the river doing cream teas and selling homemade produce, which we wouldn't be justified in patronising if we had seven days' meals already provided. I think she also envisaged us living on things out of the fields or the river, although my experience with that is that you are always neurotically afraid you've picked the very similar poisonous one, or that whatever it is boils away to nothing, or else that it's just plain nasty. I said that on the whole I preferred to be full.

I was still aware of being quite wound up. Boating acts in a different way from walking. In walking too you unwind gradually, each hour and each day feeling a little freer and more native and endued to the open air and the earth than the last. But right from setting out the physical action of walking is serving as a release. In boating you do not have that immediate means of beginning to shake off accumulated bodily cramps and mental frowsts of indoors. Unless you are the one rowing you are getting no exercise, and even if you are it is exercise of a concentrated kind. You are getting the open air to just the same extent, and intoxicating it is, especially when tinged occasionally with that compound odour of oil and rotting weed which is so delightful to a river-lover. But the element that is quite distinct, and slower-acting, is the effect of the water itself. In the womb you float, and in the cradle or cradled arms you rock, and it seems to me that one of the undoubted healing effects of being in a small boat on calm water is the re-creation of those sensations.

One of Phoebe's reactions to having time to think is hypochondria. I am differently constituted and find it easier to leave that behind on holiday.

'I've got psoriasis,' she says, holding out her hands to us, in both senses. *Mummy, tell me I haven't.*

'Oh, really,' says Emma, who knows her pretty well.

'You haven't ,' I say firmly, and as unsympathetically as I can manage.

'You said the doctor told you it was eczema.'

We remind her that J. and Co. got all that out of the way

before they left, suffering from every complaint in the medical dictionary except housemaid's knee. This by the way was something we did suffer from before the trip was over.

We went through Godstow Lock with a boatload of people from Radio Oxford, presumably just out for pleasure, although one of them has the professional nose. There is the usual banter and then he suddenly says:

'I know, you are three *ladies* in a boat, and you're going to write the book!'

They offered to give us a tow if they met us later, but we didn't see them again.

It was noteworthy that of all the many people whom the idea seemed to strike that we were three *ladies* (it was always ladies rather than women) in a boat, and then went off into peals of laughter as if they had made a huge joke, he was the only one who thought that the idea might have occurred to us for ourselves, or that at any rate he might not be the first to say it – although in point of fact he was. Probably he was an engineer or a sound man and not a journalist at all, but it set me wondering whether it represented the plus side of the learned or innate characteristic of the journalist to want to make everything into a 'story'. Maybe the hall-mark of the honourable and really useful journalist is just that, that he or she can recognise that fact is much stranger and more interesting than fiction, and *finds* the solid story rather than spinning it up out of virtually nothing like candyfloss.

I seem to be worrying away at the etymology of invention again, not for the last time I imagine. I like to spin a yarn myself, but I'm afraid of lies. Communication seems so impossibly difficult even when you are trying hard to be truthful. But there – I daresay my pre-existing animus against 'the media', its inaccuracy, its appalling power, its bogus glamour, has been fuelled by the fact that it was with two young ladies (women?) in the media that my husband and the friend who broke her wrist's husband at about the same time 'ran off', and all that had entailed a lot of lies. But there again, probably my animus should be directed against the public for being taken in – and the husbands. And there once more, they almost certainly said we didn't understand them; and for my part I admit that is perfectly true – I didn't in the least. Anyway now I come to think of it, two of my greatest heroes are journalists – Brian Redhead who seems wise and kind, and Duncan Campbell who seems brave and clever, and what is more Phoebe's boyfriend is a cub reporter and I wish to think well of his profession.

Are you thinking that I shouldn't say this kind of thing? That it's too private, inappropriate? That you don't wish to know that? Ah, bear with me ... I believe that until we can begin to own up to some of our hidden feelings we are just playing at talking to each other and running the planet. And that is such dangerous play. Of course you will say – if you can see what I'm on about at all – that I don't admit everything. Of course not: I can't see all my motives. One skin at a time. Slough them off and join me. It's lovely after the first shock. And I believe too, though how it can happen is a spiritual mystery, that it is not an impossible task of piling up pages of commentary over every word and act, because we should grow simpler after a while, and yet not feel diminished, but rather the reverse.

The man from Radio Oxford said something else:

'How far you going? Lechlade?'

'Cricklade,' said Phoebe, instantly.

'Good for you,' the man replied heartily, acknowledging something in her tone.

And how extraordinary – as I have been suggesting – the number and complexity of the thoughts that can go to make up a single word and its attendant tone! We had hardly discussed the matter at all, the general plan being to see what we felt like, and how hard the rowing proved. We were not out to prove anything, or achieve anything. We didn't need to do that: that was what men did. We wanted to spend the week on the river, we would see what took our fancy as we passed, we would turn round halfway through the week.

So Phoebe had no brief from the rest of the crew to say that, and yet in that moment our resolution began to form. I suspect Emma and I both assented inwardly; I know I did. Of course that was what we were doing. At that time we had little idea what going to Cricklade might entail, but we knew that powered boats couldn't get there, and we had already tasted once or twice the pleasant awareness that however much the launches fancied themselves as lords of the river, the more discerning types, like some of the lock-keepers, often secretly despised them, and considered that we were the true nobility. Powered boats outnumbered unpowered by at least a hundred to one, but scarcely any of the unpowered boats were going more than a mile or two, which gave our expedition even more of a cachet. Besides, perhaps beyond Lechlade we would enter a more mysterious region, quieter, more fully given over to nature. The inaccessible and unsullied began to call to us. Yet before the man from Radio Oxford opened his mouth we had been content simply to be out on the river for a week. Most people didn't seem to think we would manage that. Then by seeming to expect us to be able to do a reasonable distance, by not questioning our competence, he immediately made us feel empowered, challenged even, perhaps, though in a benign way. Phoebe's tone in replying had not been boastful, but it was clear, correcting an assumption with a slight emphasis, necessary only from the fact that her reply might be unexpected.

We discussed it afterwards. We agreed we were still keeping our options open. But the Cricklade idea was definitely afloat.

6

Beauty began to sink in a little deeper. Up to then it had
been kept at a distance by the tangle of thoughts and cares
I'd brought with me. I have learned that to look at water
and sky and foliage feeds the spirit, if you give it the
chance, but it is like rain on the earth, so that if the earth of
you is too dried up by drought it can't permeate at first.
The river is wide, and peaceful. This does me good: my
life recently has become increasingly narrow, and troubled.

It is August, and the spires of purple loosestrife are the
most striking blooms, and the first on Phoebe's list of wild
flowers, which grew to a hundred species before the week
was up. There is something very consoling in the idea of
the perennial; it speaks of persistence and hardihood and
unquenchability, and these ubiquitous tall plants with their
strong colour seem the very emblem of it. Good: I nibble at
those qualities too, hoping my strength and appetite for life
will come back bit by bit. 'Long purples', Shakespeare
called them, 'that liberal shepherds give a grosser name,
but our cold maids do dead men's fingers call them.' We
can none of us see the dead men's fingers bit, ourselves,
but perhaps you need to be a cold maid to recognise the
resemblance. We do better as liberal shepherds, and come
up with quite a few variations of grossness, though even
that needs a fairly vivid imagination.

Purple is the August colour, along the river bank. Loosestrife is brightest, but different kinds of willowherb echo it, and thistles and hemp agrimony and red clover at the edge of pastures, and mauve-tinted yarrow, and the carmine stalks of meadowsweet, and the little maroon flowers of figwort, and dark bittersweet, and the reticent, elegant pink of the flowering rush. But there are yellows too, for contrast. Loosestrife has a yellow variety, and there is mustardseed, and yellow waterlilies with their seedpods held on the slant in the water like miniature winejars. And then there the are forget-me-nots, snippets of sky, and they give me pain.

I once had the word engraved inside a ring. And there was a certain vase with soft blue painting on it, and the word again on that, and in pain at an infidelity I once took and smashed it on the ground. They look quite delicate and fragile, but they have a long flowering season, by the water. I must learn to bear their beauty and their name again. Each is like a scrap of sky with a tiny yellow sun in it. It looks at me, I fancy, neither with compassion nor with scorn, but as fact. That helps. 'The facts are kind,' writes Gerard Hughes in *God of Surprises*, 'and God is in the facts.' My reason can't tell me what that means, but it is one of the most consoling sentences I have ever read in a spiritual book, and I've devoured a good many in my time.

There is a character in one of John Cowper Powys's kindly novels who dies with the word 'Forget', rather than 'Forgive', on his lips. I think the suggestion is that that is all he felt able to ask. Powys himself, as always, reserves judgement. The hero of Hardy's deeply depressing book *The Mayor of Casterbridge* wants not to be remembered after his death. That is the extreme of the depressive minus when turned in on itself. I should like to be remembered, and remembered kindly, and before I am dead, though the ending of a love affair is a kind of death. I must then myself set about remembering it kindly. To attempt to forget is only to have skeletons, or even decomposing corpses, falling out of your cupboards when you forget and open those same cupboards again by mistake, thinking they were empty. Or it is to find yourself smashing another forget-me-not vase on another kitchen floor, and realise too late that you've been here before. To remember is to fill your house with good pictures; not pretty ones that will cloy in a day, but lifelike works of art that puzzle and hurt and sing and help you live. True to form, the last word of Jerome's autobiography is 'forgive'.

We decided to camp for the night on the lock island at Eynsham, attracted by the prospect of a proper lavatory, and a basin with hot water. Emma had been looking through one of the two handbooks that we'd brought, which had almost immediately fallen in the bilge water and which stayed wet for the rest of the trip. But she managed to decipher the passage that described these things, and they had a pleasant sound. When we got there we found the bank was two feet above us (and crumbling and nettly to boot, and even more so to bare leg and sandal) and we realised that all we had to tie up with was about two feet of fraying waxed string attached to the stern. We paddled about trying to work out what to do, and a small dour man who had a tiny gleaming steam launch already moored there put down his bucket of coal and came and sized us up. Steam launch owners are the villains of *Three Men in a Boat* but this steam launch now seemed a likeably unusual and old-fashioned survivor; just as steam trains do, and their owners likely to be harmless and knowledgeable enthusiasts rather than thoughtless river-hogs.

'That all the rope you got?' he asked gruffly, and all but clicked his tongue, which we would certainly have deserved.

Without many more words, he went to his boat, brought us a decent length of proper rope, and made us fast, both ends, to mooring-posts.

'Put it on the boat tomorrow if I'm not here,' he said, and then left us alone, a verray parfit gentil knight.

We were embarassed to be ill-equipped and to need help; but we were, and we did. We thanked him warmly. I suppose inasmuch as I'd thought about it at all, I had envisaged tying up by one end to a willow root. But willow roots much of the week turned out to be less conveniently arranged than imagination had them. And the places with mooring-pegs were all designed for launches from the high decks of which you stepped out on the level of the bank. We were appreciative at the time of the steam launch man's help, but by the end of the week we appreciated him even more. We got an extraordinary amount of uninvited male advice in the course of those seven days, and it was almost invariably wrong, or offensive, or both. Our laconic gnome proved to be the true Galahad of the river.

We were at least well-equipped and competent as regards the tent, and reasonably so in getting our supper. After that I lay down with my head on my rucksack in that extreme of relaxed comfort that comes with the cessation of physical effort combined with the satisfaction of the basic physical wants of food and bed, and abandoned myself to watching a sunset skyscape that with the usual dull business to attend to, or to imagine one needed to attend to, would have seemed quite ordinary. And of course, as even simple cloudscapes do, it proved when you gave it attention to be a mystic work of art of extraordinary beauty. Soft delicate dark grey smudges moved across even softer masses of white and cream, across a pale blue background.

Dew is coming down and we have to cover everything up. Some harvestmen have occupied the tent, which is pitched on mown hay. We evict them and lie in the tent, the girls reading, and me staring at an apricot and forget-me-not space in the cloud, an entrance, a door on the beyond. The waterproof cushions from the boat were useful to sit on while we ate, and they then became our pillows, giving that special pleasure objects give when they are versatile and you are travelling light.

It becomes apparent that Phoebe has somewhere trodden in dogshit and her shoes have to be banished outside the tent. We wipe them as thoroughly as we can and I cover them with hay to keep them dry.

'An old bush trick,' I say, absurdly pleased with myself at our being there, at our practical contrivances, at life reduced to simplicities, at coping with it.

The evening is deepening with a fiery sunset low on the horizon and a chorus of thrushes. The family fishing on the opposite bank reluctantly go home, as the terns have already done. A few late fish still leap. More unearthly by the minute, the sky deepens from scarlet to crimson. The lowering cloud hangs very low, but with singing flame red under it. A few spots of rain fall. We zip up the window and our warm bags and I sleep, right through the night as I have not done for weeks, and far more soundly.

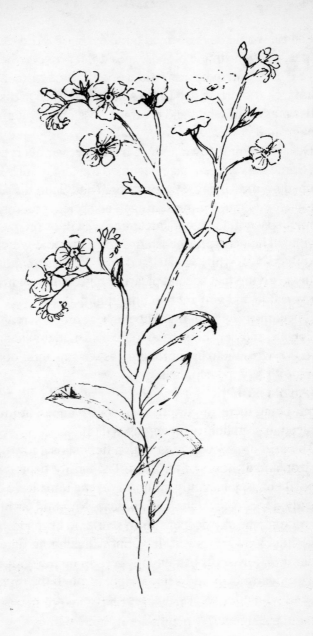

7

At six next morning we woke to hear fishermen's voices
opposite us again. I'm not sure if it is the same ones as last
night or not, but whether or not it is plainly an obsessive
pastime, and a little bit of me envies them the possession of
so strong a passion, or enthusiasm. From an upstairs
window I can often see a green umbrella stationed by the
River Cherwell for the whole of the dreariest of days. Not
that I should care to fish, particularly, unless it were to get
my dinner – an aspect they do not seem to bother about
very much; but it is the pleasure in the occupation that I see
and wish I had. Perhaps it has something to do with losing
oneself.

There has been a heavy dew and there is now a thick
mist, heralding a hot day. Huge cobwebs, creations of the
night, hang on the lock gates like gigantic thumb-prints,
covered in drops. Something bolts past along the surface of
the water, and I see it only out of the corner of my eye, see
only enough to register the manner of the movement, but
no colour. Unsatisfying, tantalising, but my first kingfisher,
I am almost sure.

Once you have seen one you can get a kind of hunger for
kingfishers, a need to see them from time to time. Where I
live, by the Cherwell, I recently went a year or more
without seeing one. A neighbour of mine who is a

naturalist told me that it was because the hard winters had killed them off. Somehow my spiritual winters were also harder without them. One day I walked my usual circuit, on a grey and windy day. Life seemed more than usually colourless, and most of the birds were skulking among the leaves and not to be seen. I sat for ten or fifteen minutes on the low-slung branch of a willow that makes a sheltered seat. Not all that long, but long enough to be staking a claim for just sitting, in the face of all the activity that my 'oughts' were wanting to foist on me, and enough to outface the false guilt that follows on saying no to them. The river had filled up with summer rushes, and reeds were growing thick near the bank, and on the bank were willows, tall grass, and nettles. Framed by the willow, and sunless, my picture was a thick but glaucous green.

And then a word came to me from years back – twenty-five years or more, and yet so small a pinch of time, so utterly, under eternity, still me – a word from my pale blue Latin 'vocab' notebook at school with its two columns, *exspecto*, I wait for. I was not expecting, not even hoping, particularly; I had looked in vain so often. I was only waiting. I may well have said in some deep part of myself, *perhaps I shall see a kingfisher today* – but if so my conscious mind was not aware of it. Then into the edge of my vision flew a bolt of burnished bronze and before my eyes could pass it to my brain to give it a name, *its* eyes and brain had tightly cornered it on seeing me and slipped it back along the way it had come with scarcely lessened speed, and for some fractions of a second I could drink blue fire.

I intently tongued the glass for every trace of it, then sat for a few minutes more, for the after-image, seeing the blue tones in that thick green world. At home I looked in a Latin dictionary and could scarcely believe what I read:

> exspecto, *to want to see, to wait; to expect with desire, fear, etc.; to look for, to long for, to apprehend;* almost *to have need of, require.*

Almost, as if half-doubtingly. Oh yes, but that's it exactly! And I would not have thought Latin could be a mystical language. It was as though Sir William Smith, D.C.L., LL.D., or perhaps J.F. Lockwood, M.A., Lecturer in Classics at the University of London, who revised the book, one of them in his systematic, scholar's search for sense had sat beside me on that old grey tree, I seeing beneath his dry exterior, he bearing with my sloppiness, and both of us knowing what it meant to be burned by that needed blue.

A mile or two down the river there is a shop and boatyard, and we are able to buy some rope of our own and and some apple juice and fruit pies, and Phoebe and Emma bought themselves each a pair of absurd pink-and-green sunglasses, with shades that flipped up. For some reason we did not buy kitchen paper, although we'd been saying we needed it on every occasion, rather as Tolkien's Sam Gamgee had felt about rope. We were proud to have our own rope, and to watch the ends being neatly and painstakingly melted together while we waited, to stop it fraying. There was something very satisfying about purchasing this basic piece of 'chandlery'; it seemed old-fashioned – the obverse of the sort of set-up where everything comes in plastic packets and you have to get some whole large unit rather than the tiny part you need. And it felt practical, and professional. It made us insiders.

Emma turns out to be able to row very nicely, almost too nicely to begin with. She's been having lessons from the woman who rowed in the eight and has learned a flashy style designed for speed where you turn the oar at every stroke. But she soon settled down to a steady, workmanlike, keep-at-it-all-day kind of stroke. For some reason her paddling style was different again. Because of the width, and needing to be at one side, we needed to use the oars as paddles when entering and leaving locks, and at such times Emma would put on a dreamy Lady of Shallot sort of look and paddle very feebly, so that whoever was wielding the other oar would have to compensate by paddling on both sides. Phoebe's rowing style was to throw herself into it with enormous vigour for the first mile, to show us how slow we were being, and then get worried that she'd done something to her spine. As for me I am erratic and get very red, but am determined to show that I have as much staying power as the girls. We row in two-mile stints.

Phoebe as map-reader tells us when our time is up, but since she once forgot, and gave one of us an extra quarter of a mile, we thereafter affect to grill her suspiciously on just how far we have gone. Actually, I think she usually over-tasked herself rather than either of us.

The heat was increasing, and it became desirable to moor up somewhere, and drink the apple juice and eat the fruit pies. A fisherman saw us try to moor by a high bank and give it up, and called out:

'There's a beach at the corner.'

We aren't sure what he means but we row on, and then sure enough there it is, a lovely stretch of pale sand where we can step out into cool water and feel it soft to our feet, and pull the boat up a gentle slope till it sticks in a satisfying way. In the sand there are tiny broken shells, and live freshwater mussels that look very appetising, but which we dare not eat for fear of pollution, and in the shallow water shoals of tiny silver fish. We eat and drink and then paddle and Phoebe swims and Emma paints, all of us taking pleasure in the place. Finally I lie very still for a quarter of an hour, experiencing the heat as blessing, seeing the sun as starry sparkles through the big-brimmed straw hat I have pulled over my face.

I've had this hat for years, and every now and then I have to re-stitch the brim to the crown, and I know I shall be very sorry if the time comes when it can't be mended any more. 'Oi loike yer 'at!', a quite small boy once said to me with that precocious flirtatiousness that sometimes goes with having to fend for yourself early. I like it too. The Greeks, who wear straw hats a lot, but usually rather flimsy ones, often said the Greek equivalent of this when I wore it there – on my honeymoon actually, and the marriage lasted for almost twenty-five years, so the hat has done well. They would exclaim over the fact that it was 'double' – i.e., stoutly made with two layers of woven straw. That seemed as strange and foreign as anything about us, in some of the out-of-the-way places we walked to, though they asked if we had the sun and moon in England, and the Virgin Mary. Our Greek was not up to theological discussion, so we assented to the third as well as to the first two, and they seemed relieved. For walking by water in particular I extol the virtues of the straw hat – your eyes are shaded from the glare, but unlike with sunglasses you still have the true range of colour.

I realise we are just across from Farmoor, where for a

year or two before my father-in-law died he lived in a
nursing home, and used I think to appreciate our visits,
although he had all but lost the power of speech. It was a
sad and a difficult time for all of us, and I sadden again,
remembering his zest for the simple things he enjoyed – his
family, food, fires, his garden and his books, and – if I'm
honest – his affirmation of me, as well as his temper and
misanthropy. Now he is dead, and my husband gone, and I
am still trying to make sense of it all, and now there is the
loss of this recent love which came all unlooked-for and
was as inexplicably withdrawn. Two lines of my friend
Jerry Hooker's ask what I want to ask:

> Where do you go,
> unspeakable love?

But alongside the sadness that has increased with realising
where we are, there is something else. It comes with the
moment or two of complete silence. The Sunday world is
becalmed, till you can just catch the sound of church bells,
very distant. The thought flashed by like a kingfisher, and I
didn't quite see it. It is something to do with this, that in so
many matters I always missed the opportunity, lacked the
imagination, as it were to go round the other side of
Farmoor, see it from another angle, and that maybe
something can still be salvaged by doing that, even if it
comes only in time to make a salve for the wound. But
maybe it has to be outside time, in holy time, in holiday
time, as Sunday can still, occasionally, seem to be outside
the week.

'You look like an Impressionist painting,' calls a man
from a passing boat appreciatively. Three women, two
young and beautiful, one half hidden by a big straw hat as

she pushes the boat out, the boat, the sunlit river and green bank ... The impression is one of happiness, and I'll damned well prove him right. No man shall drag me into the dark minus when life can be so lovely.

We pass three women sunbathing on a narrowboat. They have a strong and care-for-nobody feminist air. They look at us quite curiously – another three women on a boat, and they are *rowing* – and say 'Hi' in a friendly way. They are probably my age and I wonder whether I and my middle-aged friends would have looked like that, if I had been with them, and to what extent we imagine strength and confidence in other people. Phoebe was astonished when she realised that most of the other student teachers had felt that they were going through the mill just as she did. They'd all seemed so cool ...

Someone drives a motor boat very incompetently into the next lock and the engine smokes. We sit and inhale the poison patiently, low down and unable to escape it by getting out onto the lock. The lock-keeper looks contemptuously at the launch and prefers to talk to us. He wants to tell us that he hired a rowing boat for a fortnight thirty years ago for only £16, and he makes us feel, by his tone, obscurely censured, as though because things ain't what they used to be we shouldn't be doing them at all.

It is very hot and we do find a suitable willow where we can tie up for lunch. On getting out we find a frog in the boat and wonder if it has just come in off the bank, or if not how many miles we have brought it away from what it knows. It sits very still where we put it for a while, and we look at it rather helplessly. Perhaps it is injured, or wants to be in the water? Eventually we find it has vanished. We wished it well, but very likely we disrupted its life, inadvertently, quite significantly. We are in the main, probably even the most dedicated naturalists among us, pretty nearly as ignorant of the habits and needs of the other creatures as though we had just arrived on this planet.

And the fact is, we have become so alienated from our natural instincts that we scarcely know how to deal kindly with our own species, even those we live close to. How often we feel as impotent as we did before that frog in the face of some unexpressed longing for a need to be understood without words, or even in plain contradiction of words we actually hear. The principle of Do-as-you-would-be-done-by is not much use beyond being another way of saying that we all need love. Probably all frogs want to be kissed – and let us suppose for a moment that we are all frogs, that we have that much in common – but the kiss must not be patronising, or possessive, or ill-timed, or one of a perhaps infinite list of provisos, or it won't work. And isn't there a flaw in this anyway, in that a whole and achieved human being is presupposed, to give the healing kiss, and not just another faulty, needy frog?

How arrogant of us in any case to take another creature as the type of the ugliness that comes from being unfed emotionally, or of any other quality in ourselves that we deplore! This is scarcely an original thought, but being out of doors and glimpsing the other species getting on with their lives reminds us of the contrast between their blamelessness and the incalculable harm we do, to them, the planet and so, short-sightedly, to ourselves.

A rowing boat is a reasonably harmless mode of transport. It makes little wash, or noise, beyond the squeak of the rowlocks, and no fumes. Being low in the water it also gives a more intimate view, though the price is that you are trapped in with the fumes from the launches as you are walking in a deep Devonshire lane when cars go by. Between high banks we become denizens of the river closer to the level of grebes and moorhens, and become aware how much of their life is hidden among the reeds. Like them, when the banks are steep we cannot even see the fields to either side, and the river becomes our world, our habitat. The tall launches going by at speed, with their noise scattering most of the creatures into concealment well in advance of them, seem to relate to the river as to a motorway. They can see the countryside to right and left, though scarcely feel or experience it, and the river instead of being a various, mysterious place to be explored, with a life of its own, is merely being used as a road to master at speed.

The rowing-boat view of life is more like the child's. We are often too low down to be able get out without difficulty. But we see the life of the reeds, a child sees the life of the hedge, or the field of tall grass, while the 'grown-ups' in their launches look over the top, but miss much for that very reason.

J. and his friends had, or at any rate he fantasizes about their having, fun at the expense of the steam launches, drifting about and getting in their way and pretending to be too incompetent to get out of it. I am not sure if he would have been so bold with the huge and powerful brutes of machines – it seems absurd to call them boats – that blast their way up and down the river today. Besides which, they are so hugely in the majority that it is hard not to feel at times like a cyclist that has strayed onto the motorway. The numerous variations from the launchmen on the engine joke on us – 'Hey, lend us your engine', 'Isn't it time you changed engines?' – point up what has become normal, so that ''Oo are you a-rowing for, Hoxford or Cambridge?' from a fisherman has almost a pleasantly period ring to it.

The last two miles seem very long. This had been our first full day, and a very hot one. We are beginning to realise that as well as blistered palms and bruised bums from rowing, and bruised hips from sleeping on the ground, we have all had too much sun and are shaping up to be red and sore. Someone advises us to trail our hands in the water and let them dry, and it does seem to ease them.

We come at last in sight of some pylons. Pylons are a depressingly prominent feature of the landscape in these reaches, especially when despite your aesthetic protest you are initially delighted to see them, since the power lines are apparently crossing the river a few hundred yards further down, which means you have almost reached Tadpole Bridge where you mean to stay, only to come round the bend and find they have looped themselves up and the pylons have all moved over to stand on one bank, and you must have got at least another mile to go. They have now discovered power lines give you cancer too, if you live near them, as well as disturbing your mind with their hum and wounding your sense of beauty.

We are pretty done in by the time we do get there, and decide to treat ourselves to supper in the pub, where the sight of our own rosy faces in the Ladies Room mirror is quite a shock. I all but glance round to see who else has come in, taking a moment to recognise this blowzy creature as myself.

The first drink goes to our heads quite pleasantly – we were almost drunk already on sun and air and exercise. The boy who serves seems to be about fourteen but he chats up

Emma and Phoebe like a man while they smile indulgently as at a kid brother, and the three of us eye each other's reddening skin with some alarm. We are scarcely aware of getting back to the tent and into our sleeping bags, and are asleep before we've had time to worry seriously about whether we'll be fit to carry on in the morning.

8

Which almost, when it comes, I am not. Physically, I was in quite good shape. I was more covered up than the girls yesterday, and in any case I'm more tanned from gardening, and my palms are harder from digging. But emotionally I was low. Once again I had slept the whole night through, but this time I recalled my dream. Phoebe and Emma doubtless do not want to hear my dream, but I tell them all the same, and only as I tell them does the meaning become clear to me. I do not care for dogs, and have never owned one, never even taken one for a walk on my own. And in my dream I was given one, and because it was a gift, here I was sweaty and unrested with the trouble and anxiety of coping with it, with the falsity of trying to pretend it didn't bother me, that I really quite liked it.

'It was a black dog,' I added, and the message seemed suddenly obvious. Someone had recently lent me Anthony Storr's book *Churchill's Black Dog and other phenomena of the human mind*, in which the author described very similar dark moods to those of the man I was parted from, for which Churchill had had the metaphor of a black dog. Until I recalled aloud that the dog was black, I hadn't made the connection. And the other key word was 'given'. The fact that the dog was a gift meant a set of polite and if necessary false reactions to it. *You must not hurt people's feelings. You must always be thankful for a gift.* This alone was enough to point me to the strain of a censored reaction, but there was something else, which again I hadn't seen till I said it aloud. I have a strong philosophy of valuing The Given, by which I mean the great gift, the given things, the multifarious, odd and terrifying and lovely natural phenomena of this world, and which also means trying to accept and get on with the fixed elements in my own situation. But to believe the black dog was a real experience for its owner, and to respect its doggy space (which was hard to do at first), did not mean I was responsible for it or had to be dogged by it. And if it and its master were not to be parted, if *that* was the fact – since data are given things, and data are facts, it did not follow that I must make a dutiful third, up every morning being pulled round the park before breakfast unthanked. And I didn't care for the suburban park either, for that matter, though again I tried to learn to love it: I liked living in the country. Love me, love my dog ... ah, but I did try ...

Et cetera. I don't suppose you want to hear my dream either, especially if you hoped this would be a funny book, or a book about the Thames. But you see it is a book about this journey, and if I didn't tell you about what went on at night in my head, that was as vivid and important to me as what went on in the day, I'd be making a bowdlerising mistake as serious as the one I made over the original black dog. Not that I am so simple as to believe that I can tell you everything.

Jerome had some thoughts on that question too.

'I held,' he says in his autobiography:

that a really great book could be written by a man with

sufficient courage to put down truthfully and without reserve
all that he really thought and felt and had done ... I would call
it *Confessions of a Fool*.

And curiously enough, in another book by Anthony Storr,
the one called *Solitude*, that I had taken as my book for
this expedition, since that seemed to be what my dogged
ways had led me to, he too had something to say about
confessions, that autobiography was originally spiritual
and is now psychological.

Jerome's is a little of both, but mostly rather reticent.
The problem is that the majority of confessions involve
someone else – and I don't only mean the sexual ones –
and while that is alright in the confessional it will hardly
do in print. The only one which Jerome makes does
concern him alone. An old friend once sent him a desperate
summons and when he arrived to find her being taken to
Colney Hatch, the lunatic asylum, he not only bolted then
but never went to visit her there. Cowardice must surely
be one of the hardest things to confess, since it has none
of the glamour of the strong sins. There is no means of
wrapping it in the veil of a boast.

As a footnote to the black dog story, it was later
suggested to me that a deeper explanation was that the dog
represented the anger that I was unwilling to own. It may
well be so. Without knowing me, you can form no
judgement on the matter; but I put it in to show the Protean
nature of the truth, and how hard it is to come at even if
we think we are concealing nothing.

We'd been told last night we'd be able to wash in the
Gents at eight. Why it was to be the Gents rather than the
Ladies, was unclear, but we weren't going to be sexist

about it. Any washroom would do, but finding that neither was yet open by half past did nothing to shake off the black dog. I fulminated over this, rather disproportionately, which with hindsight I can see supports the angry interpretation of my black dog. We pee-ed in the bushes and I washed in the tent. The other two didn't bother. We tried again just before leaving and found the Gents open and unoccupied, but then hearing someone, presumably a Gent, come in to use the pissoir while we were there, we had to lurk silently in our cubicles until we judged he had gone out.

It was raining on and off, though not heavily, but it stopped for us to have breakfast – rather to my surprise, prepared that morning for a hostile world. Tea and muesli and scrambled eggs restored my temper a little. Food and physical comforts like running water and hot tea and keeping dry take on the stature of enormous blessings on a trip like this. And as life becomes simplified, my complex emotional ills begin to resume their proper perspective, as the side-effects of 'civilisation'. On simmering down, I realised that the Genial Landlord was probably just overworked and forgetful, as you're tempted sometimes to think that God must be, when blessings come too late.

Two men insist protectively on helping to cast us off, and one assures us that it will get hot again, 'temperature of 78°'. He is quite certain about this, and delivers it like an oracle. At present it is agreeably cool, but we sigh and hope it will last an hour or so at least, and row off with the river to ourselves. It is as though the launches were a kind of large white butterfly that only flies on sunny days. In fact we realise that it may have something too to do with the fact that today is Monday, and relish the thought of the quiet weekdays ahead.

We row into Rushy Lock feeling very small, the only boat. 'I've heard of three *men* in a boat,' says the lady lock-keeper. 'They filmed it here. Where's the dog?' *Don't remind me! Left behind, I hope ...*

Going up the locks you have the sensation of entering the jaws of death. They close behind you and you sit by the cold, wet, fetid wall, and hold on to the heavy, slimy chains, your warm flesh relucting at the touch. You need to hold firmly but in such a way that you run no risk of your hand being scraped or crushed against the wall. As the water comes in your boat bobs about like a leaf, and you grip the cold iron for grim life. It seems to take a long time, and you are scarcely aware of progress, though you know you must be rising. Then little by little the warmth and light increases, until behold! you are once again in the world of the living, among the bright flowerbeds of the lock, which were invisible before. The gates swing open for you and you paddle free ... It reminded me of some well-known lines of Virgil that I chose to commit to memory at school. I understand better now why they thrilled me so, not only because of some particular message for me at the time, but because they pass that high poetic test of being true on every level:

> ...facilis descensus Averno
> noctes atque dies patet atri ianua Ditis;
> sed revocare gradum superasque evadere ad auras,
> hoc opus, hic labor est.

So of course Latin is capable of mysticism, like any other language:

The descent to hell is easy. By night and day the door of gloomy Pluto lies open; but to retrace one's steps, and make one's way once more into the upper air – this is the labour and the work.

Perhaps they should bring people suffering from depression here in boatloads, for therapeutic purposes. I should call it unlocking therapy. Of course, coming back downstream and being lowered into the locks might undo the effects, though not totally, for you still have the experience of being freed at the end.

Rounding a corner beautiful with waterlilies and flowering rushes we pass two men in a rowing boat, looking extremely fed up. As we cross I take in the fact that they have gear in their boat for more than a day, and realise that they may have useful information.

'How far have you been?' I call after them as the distance widens between us.

'As far as Kempsford,' they say. 'It took us six hours. It was too weedy, we had to turn back.'

Kempsford is between Lechlade and Cricklade. Our resolution hardened: something about their failure convinced us it could be done. At least we would get that far, we said, as far as Kempsford. But inwardly we had set our sights on Cricklade.

'There are only two of them,' we told each other, to excuse our competitiveness. 'That makes a difference.'

Just beyond Radcot Lock we tied up for coffee, and watched the swallows skimming the water and in underneath the jetty where we were sitting, and rested our bottoms gratefully on the springy mown yarrow of the bank. It was still grey and windy and the sky showed no sign at all of the predicted sun. The shining damselflies, miniature kingfisher and emerald fires, were nowhere to be seen. Yesterday they had been everywhere, flying coupled with their brown mates, part of the ecstasy of heat. But we noticed bees at work on the flowers of Himalayan balsam, another contributor to the purple range, a recent but now very dominant plant in these reaches, having naturalised from gardens. And we passed a large group of Canada geese on the bank, which by coincidence have the same sort of history, and have only relatively recently been admitted as a genuine wild species.

These things are all relative. There are people who still do not feel at home with the sycamore, which was introduced in the eighteenth century. But sometimes it is more than changing one's eye. The mink is a very troublesome new species here. During the whole week we did not see a single water vole. Ratty, the pleasant, familiar companion of those who mess about in boats, is quite gone from the Upper Thames, and these bold, sleek, predatory mink are to blame – to blame too for the sharp decline in the numbers of moorhens, and of other species. Word has it up the river that 'It was them animal rights people' who unwisely let them out of the mink farms to play havoc in the wild, and it seems they were indeed responsible for some mink being released, but others escaped by their own efforts. They are difficult creatures to contain. It was the importation and farming of mink in the first place that led to this impoverishment of the river, and sad to say the willingness of women to be dressed in the humiliating garb that usually marks them as a rich man's possession.

It is not the mink that is the most 'successful' species but our own. We succeed wherever we go in damaging and destroying, acting much of the time in blind ignorance and carelessness of the consequences of what we do. And even where the damage we do is not entirely irreparable, the restoration is so long a process compared with the destruction. Thomas Hardy watched a tree being felled and was appalled to think of 'Two hundred years' steady growth' being 'ended in less than two hours'. And Hopkins' poplars, back at Binsey, he lamented both in themselves and as examples of the unthinking wounds we make in nature, 'how we hack and rack the growing green'. What a gap, what an absence, the once familiar, loveable water vole makes! The reintroduction of species is a difficult and costly business, and in any case with the mink still at large it would merely be to increase their restaurant facilities. Quite large numbers of the mink have been trapped, but they breed easily, and there seems no question now of eliminating them altogether.

Hunting them, crowds of people and dogs pursuing a single terrified creature, is a useless way of approaching the problem. Indeed it is worse than useless for it gives a pseudo-respectability to the communal satisfaction of blood-lust. I have looked into the hard faces and glinting eyes of the mink hunters who want to come across my garden and seen more than the hostility of opposed ideology; I have seen that at such time as society should sanction it, as it does the hunt, I could be as the mink, reduced to less than the status of a fellow-creature, as 'witches' have been, as women, as Jews ... 'All cruelty has its roots in lust,' pronounced Jerome with unaccustomed certainty and seriousness. It is there as a manifestation of the minus, and it only allows the minus to swallow more of life if we dwell on it. But naivety will not defeat it.

Knowing it is there in us as a species, learning the skills of opening the windows and doors of that dark dripping noisome prison, letting the healing sunshine in and the poor torturers and their victims out, this is the labour and the work ...

9

Phoebe is testing a piece of pasta from the saucepan. It is
still too hard. Emma is painting, with a pencil behind her
ear. She dips her brush in the river. I have my notebook
open, but feel discontented. Painting suddenly seems
immensely practical, and physical. At the end you have
something physical to show for it. A picture or a dish of
food, it is all one; and people will find it to their taste or
not. If they do, they can be nourished by it. But *words!*
They have no real existence; they are shadows,
approximations; they shift in meaning, they mean too
many different things to different people, *they can lie* – this
is the nub of it perhaps.

> Hamlet: I did love you once.
> Ophelia: Indeed my lord, you made me believe so.
> Hamlet: You should not have believed me. We are arrant
> knaves all, believe none of us.

Myself, I can't see how not trusting him would have
helped. Hamlet's deep mood of cynicism and pessimism
obviously hurts him.

'You are merry, my lord,' comments Ophelia
doubtfully.

'O God, your only jigmaker,' answers the anguished
man, 'what should a man do but be merry, and my father

died within's two hours.'

He is horribly twisting the true meaning of merriment by his bitter fooling.

Better to be hopeful and trusting since the other attitude hurts anyway. And who in any case knows better than I how other people's words, written and spoken, have been friends and wise counsellors as well as deceivers? Thus I struggle to reason myself back to life. There is a proper self-criticism, but this disgust with the tools of one's trade, and the trade's worth, are tyrannous taxations by the minus.

Phoebe tests another piece. It is almost done, but not quite. There is a soft vexed exclamation from Emma, who has dropped her paintbrush into the river mud and now can't find it. She carries on in ink.

So best to believe that words can be trustworthy, can throw a bridge from bank to bank across the rivers that divide us, can make sturdy, shapely, friendly little boats to carry us for a while on the water, and not let life's pain persuade us pain is all that exists.

Jerome one day found an old notebook – so his story goes, and whether it is fact or fiction is not important – containing the records of meetings of a group of friends who proposed to write a novel in collaboration. He decided that the reasons for the failure of the project, both humorous and serious, and the substance of their deliberations, would make an interesting book. He published it under the title of *Novel Notes*, but first asking permission of the friends concerned. Some words in the reply from the man he calls Jephson struck me at first as the apotheosis of purity and wisdom:

'What a man thinks – really thinks – ', Jephson is

supposed to have said, 'goes down into him and grows in silence. What a man writes in books are the thoughts he wishes to be thought to think.'

Oh, that stuck deep! What a noble simplicity it had, how it showed up one's evasive, self-protective, meretricious feigning ... Looked at more closely, the pronouncement is both cynical and judgemental, and results in a silence that is the reverse of humble.

Phoebe calls to us that the lunch is ready, and Emma shows us a picture of the boat, with a background of a clump of Himalayan balsam, and both productions are good and cheering. I receive gratefully. I allow them to begin to fill my emptiness. Besides, cooks want diners and artists want lookers, and at least I can eat and look. At the moment I have nothing beyond that to give. My few words of biro scrawl would mean nothing to anyone yet.

And now, expanded, set in some kind of order? Any sense, any salve? Any hope that one journeyman or woman can be understood by another? One thing I seem to be learning on this trip is that there is an inner ecology as well as an outer, and that the emptiness of the river throws some light on my own. I have let a single insatiable passion dominate, and like the mink it has devoured much of the shyer, more innocent fauna in me.

It is not my turn to row, and after lunch I decide to walk for a while. Here there are wide flat pastures with cattle and sheep, and it feels good to stretch my legs for a while and remember that I am a two-legged, land creature again, and to have a wider view.

The towpath could no longer be used for towing, there are too many bushes and reeds that would get in the way of the rope. But for much of its length you can walk beside the river, though in one or two places the selfishness and misanthropy of the landowners means a long detour by road.

One uses these sharp words but they seem blunt instruments. I have sometimes wondered if there were not a quasi-medical condition, so common that we take it for a normal state, to which land-owning makes people prone. Do they not suffer from an enlargement of their privacy? Why else should it be urged as a serious argument against a public footpath, as I heard it urged at a recent public enquiry, *that it passed within half a mile of the great house?* It happens that I have a footpath within yards of my window, and as it happens I like it being there. But suppose I disliked to see my neighbours walking by, no-one would take me seriously if I were to ask for it to be diverted half a mile away. Why not? Because I am not Lord Taplin, owner of guns and pheasants and stocks and shares?

Twice recently I have had the experience of having large dogs sent to bark at me when I was walking peaceably with a friend along a public path. In one case the dogs were released by an invisible hand from the house some distance away, and in the other the owners were in the garden, and we heard the injunction 'See 'em off' in a tone that could hardly have been stronger if we'd been advancing up their drive in stocking masks.

Jerome's hyperbolical denunciation of such people, which culminates in Harris's fantasy of killing not only them but all their friends and relations and singing comic songs over their graves, is a wonderful release of the negative feelings that arise in the face of the absurdity of people's pretence of possessing the earth. And there's that vintage scene in which the three of them continue eating

when they are told they are trespassing, and offer the
accuser a piece of bread and jam. Of course this kind of
staunchness is easier if you are three men, one at least of
whom is as solidly built as Harris. And of course in reality
it's costly to stand your ground, and there's no built-in
humour to take the sting out of things. But the attitude is
such an inspiring one. It's worth a whole course of
assertiveness training. The thought of it often quite
heartens me as I steal through the stolen countryside trying
not to feel as though I were the thief.

Huge planes are taking off out of nearby Fairford.
Fairford is a quiet, rich Cotswold wool town, rich in beauty
and in history, as well as that rather complacent Cotswold
prosperity, with an extraordinary set of mediaeval stained
glass windows in the church, from Creation to Judgement,
and then, close by, the base for these monstrous planes.
With their sinister pointed noses they look like a nightmare
fantasy of a stinging insect, the hum become a roar. I
remember that W.H. Hudson somewhere refers to barbed
wire as 'man's devilish improvement on the bramble': the
same negativity is at work, and in fact these bases are
always surrounded by miles of barbed or razor wire, often
in angrily profuse tangles.

There seem to be great numbers of huge planes today.
Are we always feeling this defensive? Or have they
decided we need another war, while we have been out of
touch with the news? The amount of fuel each of these
braggadocio sallies must consume is already a warlike act
against the planet. The amount of noise they generate is
already a warlike act against this country's peace.

I reflect that the things we do out of insecurity make
ugly marks – these planes and everything to do with them,

the dreary bases and the getting of their oil, barbed wire and notices telling us to KEEP OUT, pylons and motorways and everything that says aggressively, *We are not weak, we pink and wormlike things, we can have power*. And we set black dogs to bark at the stranger or the poor man at our gates. The things we do out of love and trust are far less visible and audible – the narrow path that loses itself in the grass, the wood that has been sensitively managed, the unobtrusive boat without an engine, that affords the means to go by water, for business or for pleasure, but without disturbance. All the kisses and small thoughtful acts and tender words that keep a marriage together are as invisible as growth; but the noise and ugliness of a marriage ending is often audible and visible from afar.

We are trying to prove we are powerful and on top, with our big planes and our big cars and our big boring white launches. We men sit on the top with our women and delude ourselves that we have equipped ourselves with what life has to offer. And the wash from our boats alters the ecology of the river. The life of insects we have never noticed is disturbed, and they cannot breed, and the birds that would have fed on some of them cannot feed. The more we try to possess the world the more we reduce it, the duller it becomes, and the more damage we have to do careering about it and trying to tell ourselves life is exciting in this diminished world with less variety, less beauty and less quiet. Our emptiness and the emptying world are one.

But look, the teasels are coming into bloom, with a soft empurpling, another variation on the colour scheme but with a different character, a different beauty of form, taking its place in the picture. Look at the plaited bark of the willow that has taken so long to grow and echoes the patterns made by running water, and the muscles in the body of a mammal. It seems good to believe that love has woven these, and feel the true flow and tendence of our sap and try to let it shape our floating words.

The cool, strong willow is one of the most ancient trees, older than us by many million years, can we not learn a little reticence, a little modesty, by looking at the willow, a tendency to match the flow of things?

At Grafton Lock I watch the boat go into the lock, looking smaller and frailer than ever seen from above.

'Ooh, I wouldn't like to have that thing, would you?' a lady from one of the launches says to me with a little laugh, and then trails off in some embarassment as she realises I am connected with it. I take no offence in any case – the remark was thoughtlessly made and the tone contained no malice. But still there was in it that strange and significant admixture of fear and scorn of the haves for the have-nots. The comment is ostensibly about comfort and status, but there is something else. Set us all naked in the world, both we of the tent and open boat and the pampered ladies of the launches, and we look like the likeliest survivors. And she does not think it quite nice to have to think either of such nakedness or of the overthrown world where that would obtain.

'Oh come, you exaggerate,' says the well-constituted reader, who is well-adapted to the world.

You think so? I think not. Because I too fear the revolution that would take away my slothful ease, and fail at my time of life to re-educate me in practical love of neighbour and physical and mental competence in surviving. It is so much easier not to bother, to bandy ideas

over a few bottles of wine, more than enough to be merry –
enough to dull the conscience.

10

And the thought of revolution brings me to William
Morris. We are coming, along with a tufted duck or two,
between willows, past teazels beginning to add their
purple flowers to the August chorus of purples, up to
Kelmscot, which Morris called 'a heaven on earth'. He
was referring partly to the beauty of Kelmscot Manor and
its surroundings, but he was one of those rare spirits who
seem able to set their wills to actually bringing about a
heaven on earth and keep them there. Rarer still, he did it
largely by means of affirmation. He set about living as
though in a better world, a task that is infinitely harder
than is mere denunciation or mere theory. He had an
extraordinary vision of a shared world, and we do him
and that vision wrong by letting him be reduced to the
designer of up-market cushion covers.

Not that his fabrics were of no importance: the making
of beautiful things using the unsurpassable natural
forms and colours of plants was an essential part of the
integrated life he proposed. But I think that to buy and
sell the reproduced fabric and not to try to understand the
deep spiritual and moral roots of his aesthetic, or attempt
to live the integrated life of which it is a sign is to do his
cause a disservice. Morris's vision was of a shared and
loving world where beauty would be a sign of health – on

every level – rather than wealth.

The beautiful grey house near the river where he and his friends came to live and work still stands. It is open occasionally, and if you can work out when, and can cope with the somehow conservative air that seems inseparable from the private and the public thus uneasily together, it is worth a visit. Morris has brought the river into the house, the loveliness of its willow leaves on the walls, and a verse about it embroidered on a bed hanging.

The difference between his vision and the social and economic set-up we have today is probably greater now than it was then and not less. It is very hard to estimate that, especially as we now have to think increasingly on a global scale. In the long run that may be a good thing, though at the moment it makes us feel more powerless. There is much going on in what we broadly term the Green Movement that Morris would have applauded, and matters concerning the environment are steadily in the news, and getting harder to marginalise as their impact becomes more obviously harmful to our own species. But the roots of environmental problems in our attitudes show little sign of changing. We still look for cures for symptoms and not the radical changes that would make for health – and will do till enough of us choose to order matters otherwise.

The difference between Morris's vision and what we have pains me almost more than the thought of the unhappiness in his love life, though I can empathise with that. He probably sat by the river here, just where I am sitting, and felt that he might drown through sheer heaviness of heart. But even in the bright world of *News from Nowhere*, where he describes a society in which work is undertaken for love, and people live balanced and fulfilling lives in fellowship, he still allows that mismatches of affection are the one incurable thing that might cast a cloud. I have tended to believe that unhappy relationships and broken marriages are one of the signs of our more general failure of community. But whether Morris is right on that or me is less material than what he makes me see: there is work to be done that is not dreary slogging, but fulfilling, properly human work. This is the labour and the work, to carefully save the small seeds of beauty and affirmation and nurture them. It is work that may be attended by many failures, and it isn't easy, but it is its own reward. Jerome said the same thing, that we are here for work not happiness; but seeing how life-affirming his work was, and knowing that he did enjoy a measure of happiness, I think he must have meant that we can always do our work, and happiness may come but is not ours to choose.

Phoebe and Emma have gone to look at the outside of the house, and into the church which in the book he has reclaimed for communal feasting, and as I have seen them before I stay with the boat and with Morris for company, trying to figure it out. Some of the characters in *News from Nowhere* rowed down from London – a transformed and clean and beautiful London – into the still deeper beauty of the Upper Thames. They came to enjoy the healthy and delightful work of harvesting the hay.

What would have changed just here, since Morris's time? The countryside is emptier of people and flowers. Although there are so many people out of work, I can see no-one here working on the land. Ah, there's someone herding the cows – in a tractor – to where they will be milked – by a machine. And these dull and virtually odourless grass fields would then have been full of the sweet and varied scents of meadow flowers. In his book Morris wipes away ugliness and want and shows the world as he thinks we could make it if only we'd choose to do it. It is so reasonable a way to live, acknowledging that self-interest and that of the community cannot be opposed, that the exercising of our own true gifts must be for the common good. And yet look at this gate. There might once have been something there both beautiful and made to last, something someone had taken pride in making. There is so much solace in beauty, that it seems the oddest self-inflicted punishment that we don't seem to care more to create, and instead so carelessly mar what exists in nature. I find ease in looking at the delicately pale blue flowers of the plant called skullcap, and the grey rosette of a thistle, despite having pricked myself on it. It is like a magnified snowflake.

Morris would have seen neither launches nor pylons nor the planes that are built like parodies of stinging insects, nor the war-time pill-boxes that line the river in these reaches. Out of curiosity I went into one when I was on the towpath, wondering if they would do for overnight shelters, and found it full of rubbish and a stench. Obviously some messy members of my species had the same thought.

We couldn't at first work out the strategy.

'I think they thought the Germans would come up the Thames,' I said.

'I can only suppose they weren't rowing,' said Phoebe practically, eyeing the slit with some suspicion. Boats certainly were an easy target, and it was hard to see how they'd have got past the first one.

'Perhaps there are armoured boats, like tanks,' I next suggested, doubtfully. Later I read that they were to prevent the enemy from *crossing* the river. Fortunately of course it never came to that. Meanwhile the pill-boxes are an ugly monument.

The willows that Morris so loved are an emblem of hope to set against our concrete and our steel. The sudden speaking creaks and groans of the crack willow make them seem the most animate of trees, and they must be one of the most persistent things in nature. A huge one at the bottom of my garden blew down once in a storm, and brought down the electric cable with it, cutting off the entire village. The logs from it gave a good three years of fires. And now the stump has sprouted a hedge of willow as high as the house. Plant a stake of willow and it will burst into leaf. There are several different species that tend to mix, but they all combine strength and grace. The slender shapely leaves set off the rough and often grotesque trunks. We pass an extraordinary one that has a divided trunk – it must be joined underground, for it grows as a single trunk from a few feet up. It is all the more shocking for looking like one of us. But mostly they split and twist and grow at every angle, softened and clothed by the cool green speary leaves.

When the sky was blue and the sun hot the water looked blue and smooth. Today it has been ruffled and it looks grey, and we notice the aspens more than anything else, with their sad grey colour and the sad sound of their leaves. The whole aspect of the river alters with the weather, and it affects our mood. We row along towards Buscot Lock in the grey evening and Phoebe sings a song about an unfaithful lover, and Emma sings a long mournful ballad about lovers who die.

We realise we all need supper and our friendly tent, a home in this sad world. This is our first night on our own, and Emma remembers a horror film she watched and then wished she hadn't, and we worry for a while, remembering the boat lady's advice, about whether in this instance the towpath side or the other is the safer. There is a road not far from the other side, so we opt in the end for the towpath, despite its being fenced with electric wire. We all eye it warily as we unpack, and then Emma inadvertently stumbles against it and we find it's not on, which is one less thing to worry about.

The breeze is getting up a bit, but we get the stove to light and make supper of rice and reconstituted dried vegetables. When it comes to tea though we find the gaz cylinder has run out and we haven't another. This means no tea in the morning either, which is a blow. We promise ourselves a cup of coffee 'out', which is a small luxury we all enjoy, when we get to Lechlade. Emma and Phoebe walk off to find a pub, and I am left to my reflections. Mild apprehensiveness at being alone is far outweighed by the pleasure of solitude, and of lying here fed and comfortable, with no real or imagined duties except to come back to full life. I read Storr a little, and curiously he too – odd how things come in bunches – says work and not a relationship can be a good basis for life. Hm. It is bracing but very bleak, and I am still not quite convinced. I am glad to see the two merry faces back again, and we all settle in for the night, with an owl hooting. Lechlade early tomorrow, and then ... Beyond.

11

I woke suddenly in the night. My first thought was that
something had happened to the regulation of the water, or
that our tent had somehow got up and moved itself rather
closer to the weir. Then it came to me that this roaring was
due to the wind in the nearby row of tall aspens. The
breeze that had been blowing all day had turned into a
quite strong wind, and the always restless trees were in full
spate.

Phoebe, who was lying next to me, was reared up on her
elbows, listening; and then I too became aware of the noise
that was nearer at hand, a kind of rythmic scrape or rustle,
very close indeed – just outside the tent it seemed.

'What was that?' I said softly, trying to sound interested
rather than panicky, though I didn't pull it off.

'Did you hear it too?' Phoebe responded in a thoroughly
alarmed tone.

We both lay reared up and straining our ears. It was
horribly born in upon us that our best course was probably
to stay where we were, and hope that whoever it was
would simply steal the boat, or let down our tent for a
laugh, and then go away leaving us unmolested; whereas to
crawl out in our nightdresses saying 'What the hell do you
think you're doing?' or 'Who goes there?' though showing
some spirit, and possibly even being easier than lying low,

would only be to draw attention to our female vulnerability.

'Oh, it's just the wind,' I said with all the casual conviction I could muster, and lay down.

For some reason my maternal instinct dictates that reassuring Phoebe is the prime task, and this helps me to cope with my own panic. I remember sitting with her, then aged about eight perhaps, in a two-person chair-lift at Alum Bay, on the Isle of Wight. As we swung out over the trees and I realised that this was a dreadful mistake but that there was no going back, and that the next few minutes would somehow have to be endured, I am convinced that it was only the thought that Phoebe must be got through the experience that made it possible for me to keep a grip on myself, and on the bar of the otherwise open chair. I talked without stopping about how it was soon going to be over, how it was best to look at things far out rather than below, about how she must sit perfectly still ... As it was, in that case, Phoebe was quite unaffected and wanted to know why I was going on like that, and was all for going 'Whee! Fun!' if my obvious terror hadn't repressed it. But in the present instance I could feel her fear, and I lay pretending to be unconcerned, although longing to rear up so as to listen better and feel fractionally more ready to ward off attack.

I also told myself it could not possibly be what it sounded like, which was a man in waterproof trousers walking slowly round the tent.

Once years ago when I was a student I had gone strawberry picking as a holiday job, and had a similar scare. It was an instructive two weeks altogether. People might have studied us and then gone away and written theses on the effects on different temperaments of being subjected to a particular set of physical conditions, a certain kind of political economy. We were far out in the wilds of Cambridgeshire, flat lands with little cover, so there was no need to fence us in. The farmer had picked us up in his land rover from the nearest large town, and we had no means of getting away by public transport. As well as the farm he owned the only local shop, and received back most of our paltry earnings for overpriced, packaged food. Most of the rest of what we earned was spent on mild (bitter was unknown in those wild parts) in the local pub where we spent the evenings trying to drown our sorrows – as exploited labourers classically do – and uttering cries of anguish at the pain in our backs whenever we had to stoop once more to pick up a dropped dart.

Legend had it that on the gang before ours a man had run amok one day, and had gone out at dawn and trampled up and down the rows. One of the things that kept us going was the jester of the party, a most merry character who was always managing to make us laugh despite our aching backs and rankling sense of injustice. The irony was that he was also a very slow picker, and since we were paid by results he would end each day with even less profit than the rest of us. We would gradually leave him further and further behind, and then overtake him again, going up a new row. I have often thought since that if we had had any decency we should have rewarded his valuable role as jester as they do in Shakespeare's plays, and that he might then have received more like his due. I have forgotten his name, and have no idea what became of him; but if he ever reads this and can recognise himself I hope he will get in touch – merry hearts seem less common than they were.

But perhaps that is only growing older. Wherever he is, I hope life hasn't saddened him too much.

I say, if we had had any decency, but of course it was the result of such a regime that we all felt we would grab the largest bowl of porridge, or whatever else was going, if we could. There was a short-haired man – at a time when students wore it long – with a white polo-necked sweater, and a distinctly military air about him, who acted as our leader. Whether this was simply his natural role, or whether he received some privileges and was appointed by the farmer, I cannot now recall; but he enjoyed the job. He made out rosters for the cooking, and hounded us out of bed for the pre-breakfast stint of picking with zealous punctuality. Doubtless he is now bearing the white man's burden somewhere, or teaches games at a public school.

We slept on straw mattresses in two barns, very primly segregated, males and females, in a way that I'm sure no-one bothers with now. The other occupants of the female barn were three evangelical Christians. They read their Bibles by torchlight, and smiled the smiles of happy martyrs at the way we were treated. If the thing had been a way of life and not just a fortnight I'd have had a bleak prospect indeed: I am sure that a plot to overthrow the farmer and run the place as a commune, or making an escape plan, or even trying to form a union would have been divinely interdicted. As it was their saintly pity for the one who was not saved was pretty trying.

But one evening they had to stretch a point. Our lights were not long out when we heard the noise of heavy steps going round the barn, and a heavy body bumping into it, and even, most horrible of all, heavy breathing. We alerted each other, terrified, and took counsel in whispers. Prayer was tried, but man or devil, it didn't shift it. Finally my idea prevailed, which was that we should seek shelter in the men's barn. I could see it tried their consciences sorely, but in the end they buttoned themselves to the necks and we ran, in a body, and burst in on the men, probably scaring the wits out of them. I often wonder whether those girls plucked up courage to confess to their husbands, who were certainly churchwardens and missionaries and so on, that they had once, while yet virgins, spent the night in the company of young men.

The culprit in that case had turned out to be a cow, and I had hopes that this would prove to be the explanation now, despite the electric fence having been switched off, and there being no sign of cows when we went to bed. But it seemed too furtive for a cow.

It seemed more like the footsteps I had heard one night after my husband had left, walking up to the door in the small hours, and then silence, during which they could be imagined silently proceeding round the house on the grass. I had stood shaking for perhaps five minutes and there was then a hideous cry. At this I knew I had to dial 999, and when the police arrived they fortunately found the culprit. Having heard nothing while I waited, my next worst fear was that they would fail to do so, and put me down as hysterical. One officer came to the house, and the other drove down the lane, and they kept in touch by walkie-talkie sets, just like on *The Bill*. It was quite exciting.

'There's a car down here, broken down, do you think the old lady could have got confused and thought it was an intruder?'

'It's not an old lady,' my man said, with an apologetic look at me, 'it's a middle-aged lady, and she knows what she's talking about. Ask him if he came up to the house.'

Beyond my house is nothing but a sewage works, but for some reason it is a favourite spot for lovers. Steering toddlers past the litter of 'pretty balloons' – Eeyore's trophies that one hopes in this case have not exploded – is quite a skilled job. Probably there is some good scientific reason for it – perhaps the smell is aphrodisiac? For myself I can scarcely imagine a less romantic spot; and it's an abysmal bit of road that has meant that more than one couple, over the years, has come to the door at midnight blushing or brazen, to ask whether there is a tractor they can borrow, or if they can phone their friend's friend that runs a garage.

The man confessed to having come up to the house, and had then presumably felt unable to knock. The hideous cry was never explained, but I figured it must have been when he stepped into the knee-deep puddle that forms under the railway bridge, and serve him right. My manless state gave me a double animus – against lovers as well as intruders.

On the present occasion I somehow, quite soon, went back to sleep. At home in my comfortable bed I had been lying half-awake with the World Service on half the night; in the open air and on the hard ground and after a day's rowing it seemed I could even sleep with someone outside who was going to do us in with a tent-peg, like Jael and Sisera in the Old Testament.

Next morning I got up at dawn for a pee and found that the tent was still fastened down, the boat still in its place, and no-one around except a duck or two. At half past seven even the ducks had gone, and it came on to rain hard. We reached the conclusion that the man in waterproof trousers must in fact have been the sound of the black plastic bag that shrouded our outside belongings, being moved by the wind. We sat in the tent reading and eating bread and honey and drinking cold water and thinking rather gloomily that it looked set wet for the day. But by half past nine, before we had made any decision about whether or not to row on anyway, it stopped, and we packed up and went on down to St Johns Lock in good spirits. It was windy and grey, with masses of rain cloud, but the wind won, and as things turned out we had had the last rain of our trip.

'You're doin' it the hard way – the *proper* way,' said the lock-keeper approvingly, and we passed through the highest lock, past the reclining statue of Old Father Thames with heads held high.

But Phoebe was rowing with the rather energetic stroke she always uses to begin with, and a very classy lady on a launch called out:

'That's how we started our boating, thirty-five years ago.' She obviously meant to encourage us, but I wondered inwardly if I still had thirty-five boating years to go, and felt quite clear that I did not intend working my way up the hierarchy to the giddy heights of *Cheyne Queen III*, and that if I did any more boating it is likely to be on just such another boat as this number five.

My plan has been to hire a paddle in Lechlade. I could picture us nosing our way swiftly and silently between clumps of reeds, taken forward by the deft, skillfully angled strokes of the paddle from the front of the boat, a picture probably based on adventure movies set in exotic places, or eco-documentaries about people studying the inhabitants of the rain forests. It also seemed, in England, to be a pleasantly outdated thing to try to do.

The boatyard at Lechlade rose to the occasion. It was run in a pleasantly outdated way, where you could, if possible, have what you wanted. There was no nonsense about *not doing* paddle hire, as I half expected. The young woman wanted four pounds an hour for it. I said that as I wanted it for two days, I would be better advised to buy it outright, at that rate, and asked her to think again. She then suggested four pounds for the whole time, and I returned to the other two carrying the paddle over my shoulder like that character in Homer, doubly pleased with myself for having succeeded in my mission and driven a cool bargain.

12

We moor our boat on the end of a line of hire boats by the old wharf. It feels once again old-fashioned and delightful, like stabling our horses while we take refreshment at an inn. We feel much more like travellers than if we had arrived by car, and more at the mercy of inns or shops to accomodate our needs. Since we'd had no hot drink that morning, we did treat ourselves to cups of coffee at this inn, symbolically a Free House, that turned out to be part of the same relaxed empire as the boatyard.

Then Phoebe and Emma go off with a long shopping list, leaving me luxuriously leisured at my outdoor table, to watch each small river event with what sometimes feels like a convalescent's interest. We have the feeling that we are leaving civilisation behind and need to make careful preparation for this expedition. Certain items were starred, meaning that if the money wouldn't cover everything, these were to take priority; or that if they weren't in one shop others must be tried, or that any desperate means might be used to obtain them. Cake, I remember, was one. Phoebe was on a diet, and Emma and I do not normally hanker for cake, certainly not what my mother always used to call 'shop cake' in a disparaging tone; but that day it seemed essential.

I wanted a sponge. Near the beginning of the trip I had

noticed a woman in rubber gloves busily scouring away at already sparkling bits of a launch for all the world as though she were in her kitchen at home, while launch man lounged and read his newspaper, for all the world as though *he* were at home, and I had looked at the scene with scorn. But after a couple more days of climbing in and out of the boat, and it filling up with leaves, and feathers, and odd bits of paper, and our possessions getting rather scattered about it and trodden on, and wet, Emma and I both discovered in ourselves a housewifely craving to springclean it.

Phoebe didn't. If Phoebe is busy, she is entirely single-minded. She will find a cup that is a little less encrusted than the others, and wipe it cursorily with her sleeve, and stick a fresh tea-bag in it, and get on with what she is doing. The same goes for if she is relaxing.

'I'm on holiday,' she would argue. 'I don't want to wash up, on holiday.' She has a real genius for living. I am trying to learn it. At home I let the house go hang for days and days, fancying I am engaged in a battle of wills with the other inhabitants. But since at the moment this usually means Phoebe, she remains cheerfully ignorant of the contest, and in the end my nerve goes and I lay about me with mops and brooms like Mrs Tittlemouse. I was once away for a week, and Phoebe confessed when I came back that she had been puzzled for a while as to where her clean clothes were, until the explanation eventually dawned on her. The fact is, though I never actually read those magazines with the model women in, a lot of other people do, and they get to you more than you realise.

So I wanted to wipe out the boat. But I also wanted the sponge to bail it with. There was a channel in the bottom of

the boat that was boarded over with a gap at either end. It
was into one or other of these gaps that the guidebook had
fallen on the first day, and now the sleeve of my sweatshirt
had trailed in it and was sodden and it also smelt of the
sickly-sweet smell of bilge-water, which is quite different
from the excitingly mixed, though polluted, smell of the
river itself.

The shopping expedition was sucessful in every article,
and we rowed off feeling well-equipped and intrepid,
superior in every point to the languid launch people we
were preparing to leave behind. We took the boat down
past huge dredging barges belonging to the National River
Authority, the curious 'Round House' at a bend in the river
which marks the Usual Limit of Navigation for powered
craft, and on past the pretty group of buildings that is
Inglesham.

The morning had worn away in Lechlade, so we soon
moored to have lunch, which included cake, and cups of
tea to inaugurate the new gaz cylinder, and to celebrate
having the river to ourselves. For this last it proved too
soon. The river had remained reasonably wide and clear
for half a mile or so, and then we came on a place where
two or three launches were moored. After that the reaches
became extremely short, and the quantity of underwater
weed increased, mostly at this point a variety with leaves
in long flat green strips. Then one more launch overtook
us, making a more than usually hideous noise because
every hundred yards or so it had to reverse its engines to
try to free the propellor from the weed. At last however it
too gave up, and we found ourselves alone.

The banks were steeper and the river narrower than at
any time before. Up to now we had been able to row, but

now the clumps of blue-green rushes were so wide and frequent that we often had to ship the oars and use the paddle. Since the current was against us, the boat often did not have sufficient momentum for the paddle to be of use, and we were then obliged to take the oars from their rowlocks and use them as punting poles. Whoever was steering would grab hold of one, and whoever was rowing the other, while the third would kneel in the nose of the boat looking for opportunities to use the paddle to help us along, or fend us off from the bank if that is where we were headed. It became a matter of swift decision when to turn from rowing to punting and back again. It was vital to stand up carefully and without falling in, or tilting the boat, but if it was not done fast we might actually lose some of the forward progress we had so laboriously made. It was warm work, even under a grey sky; if the sun had been shining as it had on that shimmering Sunday I doubt if we could have made it.

Conversation stopped, as we became absorbed in the task. In any case, we needed to save our breath. Whoever was steering was making crucial decisions that were largely based on hunch. If we headed straight for that clump of rushes with two or three strong strokes, was it just thin enough for us to be able to shoot it, or would we do better to try for a channel close to the nettly bank where we could get through but clearly wouldn't be able to row for fifty yards or so? Sometimes one or other of us would give instructions, 'Punt!', 'Pull on your left, and again', or suggest 'Let's go for that space over there'. But much of the time we were silently accomodating ourselves to the efforts of the others, trying for an intense form of co-operation, involving both mind and body, as though the boat had become a three-headed beast.

The work is very hard, but there is also great pleasure in every bit of progress, and in the concentration on the single task. At the back of our minds is the knowledge that Cricklade is still about eight miles off, and the question whether, even if things get no more difficult than this, we shall be able to get there, and get back, within our week. But we do not voice it, even to ourselves, absorbed in the task of the moment. We sweat along breathing heavily.

Things do get more difficult. Besides the clumps of rushes, which sometimes fill the whole width of the river for a hundred yards at a stretch, and the long green strips of weed, there are underwater reedbeds, and stuff like the long tresses of a river deity, and what Phoebe and Emma christen 'treacle weed' because it is treacle-coloured and hard to row through, and because of the somehow sticky sound it makes against the sides of the boat, and the weight of it if you get a swatch of it looped over an oar.

'Oh look,' I say, 'it's flowering here. It's covered in little white flowers.' I am steering.

'Bugger the little white flowers,' says Emma savagely, who is at the oars.

At one point we seem to be completely stuck in the rushes: we can't even go backwards and try to force a passage in a different place. Phoebe gets out and pulls us a few yards, and then it's her turn to say 'Bugger' as she suddenly steps in a deeper place and is wet right up to her waist. But she's got us free and has cooled off into the bargain. She clambers back in, rocking the boat wildly. 'Watch out', we shout, grabbing the sides, and we manage not to capsize, and row triumphantly clear. In these reaches a stretch where you can row ten strokes without having to ship the oars seems an extraordinary snatch of liberty.

We find that we are constantly herding swans. They obviously hereabouts are so unused to people on the river that they haven't learned the art of coping with them. They will never wait at the side to let us pass, and it seems they can only hiss and be driven on and on. Emma is worried about this, and especially about dividing families, and so trying to work out ways to leave them behind becomes another of the things we are trying to include as a skill of our progress. The swans have usually spotted the best channel, but we sometimes try another in the hope of getting ahead.

Eventually we moor for tea in a tree-lined stretch, tying up to a root at a muddy little, white-feathered swans' beach, and climb up into a field of wild flowers. It looks as though it must have been planted with flax the year before, from the number of those plants remaining, and this year been left to lie prettily fallow, a deceptively pleasant side effect of the crazy policy of 'set-aside'. Setting aside chemicals would produce the same effect and be sustainable and better for the planet's health.

Our hands are chafed with rowing, with punting, and in my case also with the steering rope which no amount of reason can prevent me from pulling on for dear life even when it is already at full stretch. Our knees are bruised from our stints of kneeling on the hard little triangular seat in the nose to paddle. And the whole of our bodies feel thoroughly exercised by punting, rowing, and constantly sitting down and standing up, and balancing ourselves. Tea is elixir of life. I won't say we thought it was what they hand out when you get to heaven, because we knew we had

to go on a bit further. But it was very good, and we all –
though none of us do usually – had it with sugar in.

13

Emma said it was like *The Lady of Shallot*. We knew the picture she meant. I'd had a postcard of it when I was at school, and I still know most of Tennyson's poem by heart, I think partly because it fed, and was fed by, my river fantasies ...

> She saw the water-lily bloom,
> She saw the helmet and the plume ...

Bah! romantic claptrap. Lancelot indeed. He'd be lucky. Stupid knights pricking all over the place and thinking they were God's gift. I began to tell myself what a bad poem it was, and to despise myself for liking it so much as a girl. To think I used to think it rather beautiful that Lancelot 'mused a little space' over her dead face. Catch me fading away on account of a man.

'Oh, I mean Ophelia,' said Emma, after I'd done quite a lot of working through this. 'The one with her floating among all the flowers.'

This was almost worse, but so it was we could see, the green lushness, the forget-me-nots and waterlilies, the willows and the reeds. And once again, a woman dying for love, having first run mad ... *You should not have believed me ...*

Pah! What a total bastard Hamlet was. Then we thought

of poor Lizzie Siddall lying in the bath for hours to be painted and catching her death of cold. *We are arrant knaves all ...* Catch us dying of love, we said, but we couldn't help sighing all the same. Emma is Engaged, not like the opposite of being Vacant, but as a devotee of True Love. Officially Phoebe thinks all that's a lot of nonsense, but I've known her sigh for a man all the same. As for me – well I'm badly wounded, but not dead. And ditto my romanticism, worse luck.

We wended our slow way upstream for another couple of hours, until we came at evening to a green lawn stretching down to the water and a notice announcing a pub we later christened *The Warm Welcome*. We thought it might just be worth asking whether we could put our tent up on the bank, and after a time the girls returned delightedly carrying three glasses of beer. The barman had said that the landlord would be back in an hour and we would need to ask him, but he was sure he wouldn't mind.

I can't decide whether the beer was better than the tea had been or not. It was different. The tea was a life-line, energy-giving with its lacing of sugar. The beer was celebratory, of the end of a hard day, and of having found a hospitable inn. It relaxed us and went to our heads. Half an hour later we went back for some more. One of the regulars said:

'Oh, Harry won't mind. Go ahead and put up your tent.'

He knew his genial host. He could vouch for him. Half an hour after that the barman appeared. We smiled at him. He wrung his hands. He was really sorry, if it were his pub ... The Genial Landlord was actually going to send us off, at this late hour, to battle with more of this difficult stretch of river.

It seemed he had a friend, further on, who ran a campsite, and he didn't want to upset him. I was not sure I believed in this, because I'd enquired before the trip and been told there were no campsites that took tents. When I'd asked what on earth they did take, I was told caravans. It seemed that often caravans felt that tents brought down the tone. And anyway if the friend was anything like landlord of *The Warm Welcome*, did we want to stay there? However, there was nothing for it – we were being moved on.

Getting back into that boat and recommencing what became now virtually an assault on the river had a pretty desperate feel to it. It put me in mind of something I read once about Ouspensky, or someone of that kidney, who had a theory that humankind were all Asleep, and needed to Wake themselves Up by making strenuous, superhuman efforts. One of the exercises he recommended, I seem to recall, was that you should go for a very long arduous walk, and then when you were fit to drop, and walked in through the door looking forward to your bath and supper, you'd be sent to do the walk again. I'd always found that a repulsively sado-masochistic idea, even when I was younger and fitter. To walk twenty miles is one thing, but to think of your walk as ten and then to be told it is even a mile or two longer is quite another, so vital a part does the prepared mind play in our stamina. Perhaps the landlord of *The Warm Welcome* was a disciple of Ouspensky.

'I've never been homeless before,' Emma said, soulfully but attempting an interested, sociological tone, as we set off in the failing light. We hadn't thought of it like that, and it didn't improve our spirits. There was a sunset sky that had a certain melancholy beauty, but we had no time to appreciate that.

We wondered, later, whether the barman and the regulars would be disillusioned, and never trust bonhomie again, and go to a different pub. But it seemed unlikely. People like to believe in the myth of the Genial Landlord, and will go on persuading themselves of its truth even when all the evidence points the other way. There is a deep-seated need to placate him and keep in with him, to laugh sycophantically when he sneers at those who are absent. A narrow religion can sometimes look like that.

The banks on either side were either impossibly high, or if we could see the fields they had cattle in them. There was nothing for it but to press on and hope for the best with the campsite. We found it, wearily made fast, and went to enquire.

We could stay. There was a nice little plat that might have been made for us just above the boat, and there were clean lavatories, and there was hot water. Phoebe and Emma could wash their hair, and I could wash some knickers. (I had forgotten to allow for there being two Saturdays.) I washed my favourite red ones and hung them on the fence. We were all smiles. Little things like this can seem to make your day when you are living the simple life. There was even a shower, if you wanted.

But apart from the fact that we rather begrudged an extra fifty pence, I have found that the appliance often proves to be a dubious blessing. Electrical showers were not invented in Jerome's day, but I should like to have read him on the subject – I feel it needs his pen to do it justice. I am convinced there is a conspiracy of silence about showers. People don't like to admit that they couldn't get the apparently simple apparatus to work, and found the arrows and blue and red zones completely baffling, and that they have been scorched or frozen or got worried that something would explode or electrocute them, and got their clothes soaked as they hung over the partition and that the soap shot off under the door. They are afraid no-one else will admit it happens to them. We settled for a good old-fashioned wash.

It was pretty dark by the time our supper was ready, but fortunately on one of the wooden buildings there was a useful outside light. We finished up with the last and best drink of a day of memorable liquid restoratives. It was an extraordinary compound of chocolate and milk and sugar and oranges and it came in a packet to which you just added hot water. Phoebe and Emma had bought it that morning in Lechlade, thinking it looked promising. I am quite sure that if you arrive latish at the pearly gates and having had a hard time on the way, as I suppose most people will have done, that they will send you to bed the first night with something pretty much like that as a nightcap. But without the additives, of course. We certainly slept the sleep of the innocent, that night. And on top of all our other blessings, we were that much nearer to Cricklade ... Perhaps, after all, there is something in the myth of the Genial Landlord. But I bought some more of the chocolate nectar when we got home, wanting to repeat my pleasure, and it tasted disgusting. Religion was ever a paradoxical thing.

14

They had got up some kind of a scratch dawn chorus, even though the official season is over by August. A wood pigeon was doing its best to sound summery, despite the grey sky. A few waterfowl were in possession of the river, which was flowing past in its common, extraordinary beauty. We had scarcely been able to appreciate the spot the night before, except as a haven of rest and human amenity. Last night we had been escaping from the river; that morning we were drawn towards it again. Classically moored beneath a willow, the simple boat lies ready, inviting us once again to enter that world of blue-green rushes and green reeds, bedecked with purple loosestrife and yellow waterlilies, the world that belongs to the leaping fish and the shy moorhens and the strong white swans.

We breakfasted on muesli and tea and bacon sandwiches and then enjoyed the luxury of washing up in hot water in a sink. My hands are particularly stiff and have to re-learn how to hold things, which is obviously to do with my urgent grip on oar and steering-line. We all have stiff thighs from our stints kneeling up in the front of the boat with the paddle. But we all felt extremely well. Even so we were quite startled by the picture of rude and bucolic health that looked back at us out of the wash-house mirror.

Phoebe hasn't mentioned psoriasis since the first day, or her kidneys, or any of the other things she has heard about and has, and Emma, who keeps her worries to herself, now volunteered, after the most strenuous day we have yet had, and the most adventurous, that she had been feeling anxious and off-colour and closed-in before she came but now was feeling relaxed and fit.

A couple of men from caravans take an interest. It is such a very neat and quiet caravan site, and everyone seems to live so much inside their vans, from where they can occasionally be glimpsed polishing things, that we feel rather gypsy-like and raffish to be sitting and cooking out of doors. Phoebe is trying to work out exactly where we are, since the site doesn't appear on the map. She asked one of the men about the road on the far side. His eyes widened:

'How did you get here then?' and then when Phoebe tells him he doesn't believe her.

'Ask a silly question,' he mutters, obviously preferring to believe his first hunch that we have fallen out of the sky. But then it must have occurred to him that goddesses probably do not eat bacon sandwiches, and swear when they drop things, and hang washing on the fence, and he feels annoyed as though we had taken him in. Then it strikes him, as his masculine superiority feels the need to assert itself, that we have most probably lost our way, if not our wits as well, and he goes off for his road atlas. He comes back with it and holds us up by trying to prove on an extremely small-scale map that we are actually not on the Thames at all, but have somehow gone wrong and are on the River Ray.

Fortunately we have a much better map, and we have,

after all, made our way, slowly, in a boat, up this strip of
water, so that it's quite hard to see how we could have
gone wrong. Even I, who have had so many damaging
years of a man knowing best, feel only a moment's dismay
at the thought of all that effort in vain, and then my sense
and confidence reasserts itself and I realise it's only a
standard English male exhibiting normal behaviour. I
believe and trust – oh, may it be so! – that Phoebe and
Emma, being of a stronger generation that has learned from
mine, didn't even experience that brief helpless plunge, or
find him - or ever find in his kind - anything worse than a
moment's time-waster.

Afloat again, we are all stripping off layers within
minutes of starting out, and back once more into the swift
switches from rowing to punting. We come on a bloated
dead sheep in the water, and then further on, three more,
drawn to their death by the attractively lush vegetation of
the high bank. Their supposed foolishness does not seem to
prevent them being expert at getting through fences.
We also see the wreck of a yellow boat in the reeds.

'The last lot that tried,' says Emma grimly.

After a while the river so narrows that we can scarcely
get an oar's stretch even where the surface is clear of
rushes. The reaches are now very short, and so we have
constant changes of scene – now a close and mysterious
wooded stretch, now a field of sweet corn above us, or of
munching cattle. Occasionally we encounter an
unexpectedly wide, open stretch without rushes, where we
can row perhaps eight or nine strokes without impediment.
The day is still grey although the sun seems sometimes on
the point of breaking through. It is humid, especially down
between steep banks as we now are, and the current is quite

swift against us, which would make it warm work on any day. After a couple of hours without any landmarks at all, in a seemingly endless hidden world of swans and silvery willows, we catch sight of the spire that must be what the guide book refers to as 'the proud Tudor spire of St Sampson's Church' which 'dominates' the town. The end, though it appears to dodge from bank to bank every hundred yards or so, is definitely in sight.

We were too intent on getting there to take in the name at the time, but now I come to think about it, I had no idea Sampson was a saint. Delilah seems to be a type of Eve, another woman who mythically carries the can, and the legend, like that of the Fall, is another guilt-inducing one for women. I suppose if we were three *ladies*, who knew our place, we should not be paddling up towards St Sampson's patch, and making him feel less strong. This is the message we've got, thinly veiled by banter or patronage, and once or twice in open mysogyny, from most of the men on the way. And among my acquaintances there are only a handful of women deludedly thinking betrayal and undermining is the way to freedom; compared to so many men.

Cricklade begins to welcome us with bankside notices telling us this is private land and we mustn't moor. It's hard to believe that many boats come past, but presumably people who have the initiative to make this journey in an unpowered boat are particularly dangerous. The final reach up to High Bridge has a fallen willow across it, and it seems for a minute or two that we may fail a few yards short of our goal. But we all get into the water and somehow heave the boat through, and then the river is very shallow, and exhaustedly, trying to watch out for the rusty tin cans and broken bottles that mark a human settlement in the late twentieth century, we push and pull the boat the rest of the way.

Someone comes up and congratulates us, and tells us what seems like a lengthy anecdote about how the army once came up here, to prove it could be done, which we are too exhausted to pay much attention to. But he kindly takes a photo of the three of us standing in the water by the boat, and then Phoebe goes off in search of the fish and chips mentioned in the guide book and which she has dwelt on fondly ever since Cricklade was first mooted, while Emma and I sit rather dazedly in the boat.

The immediate neighbourhood of the river is not inviting, and a completely pointless stretch of barbed wire makes it quite difficult to get out, so desperate for tea we light the camping gaz in the bottom of the boat. It's a foolish thing to do, but our judgement is impaired by a mixture of physical tiredness and of feeling rather pleased with ourselves.

Cricklade seems remarkably unappreciative of its river, seeming to see it mainly as a rubbish dump or a means of unwanted invasion. You would think that they would like to clear and open it a little simply for their own pleasure in rowing boats and canoes. But the English often seem oddly uninterested in their rivers: look at the dreariness of the banks of the Thames in central London, that could be bright with flowers and cafés and grassy walks and stalls. Grey, all of it, making you think of pollution and lonely suicide. And think too of the all the hundreds of miles of rural rivers to which the public has no access at all. Hudson says we should simply take it as a natural right, to walk alongside the rivers of our land, and he is morally right in my opinion. But it would not at the moment be much of a pleasure, unless physical obstruction and the expectancy of the adrenalin of confrontation is what you enjoy. I should like to walk along rivers which are still used to travel by, on paths where I should meet my fellow creatures pleasantly, where human beings are living gently with the other species.

Phoebe comes back with a large hot paper bundle and we somehow get it and her and her shoes past the barbed wire and back into the boat, and then sit and avidly shovel down our fish and chips with stiff fingers. We just manage not to have an accident with the gaz, and drink our tea gratefully, but we all seem clumsy and the boat seems more unstable grounded on the sharp rubble – not pleasant river-rounded stones – of Cricklade than it does mid-stream afloat. We all think one of the others is rocking it, and get bad-tempered with each other. The man with the anecdotes comes back, and asks how long we are going to be there, because he has asked the local paper to come. We say we shall be on our way in a quarter of an hour, and he seems a little crestfallen. We feel rather remorseful at being so unco-operative, but we can't afford to hang around while they hunt up a photographer. In any case we are soon hastened on our way by a rain of small missiles from somewhere out of sight on the gloomy bank. It is probably children, and Phoebe calls out sternly to the unseen assailants to 'Stop that at once!' and we suddenly recall the usually unlikely-seeming fact that she is a schoolteacher.

Phoebe says the other possibility is that it is the work of KBOOCA agents, which are not, as you might think, African freedom fighters, but the Keep Boats Out Of Cricklade Association. We all agree that if there is any such thing we are pretty much on their side. The idea is sometimes mooted that three more locks be made in order that launches should be able to come up yet another ten miles of Thames, eroding the banks, upsetting the ecology, polluting the water, poisoning the air with fumes and destroying the peace with noise for other people and animals alike is appalling, but typical of our species. We lack delicacy. We seem interested in complete conquest of the land or nothing. The idea of a gentle, continuous, minimal management is much more rare. And yet that is what we are going to have to develop if we want our children's children to enjoy the beauty of the earth.

It is time to begin our journey home. We hope they won't tap their foreheads and smile when our friend turns up with the newspaper people and finds no trace us, and he swears he *did* see three women in a boat. Fortified by our lunch, but still awkward at doing something we haven't tried before, we pull the boat round, and stumble anxiously along, fearful to the last of cutting our feet, and then clamber in as it takes the water, going, for the first time, downstream.

15

And oh, the bliss! After all the effort we are so inured to making, the pleasure in feeling the current take us is extreme. We had hoped it would be a little easier, but hadn't anticipated anything like this. The joy of gliding forward so swiftly after every stroke or push, of going with the stream, seems to carry some message for our lives. We certainly wouldn't appreciate it as much if we hadn't done the hard part first; perhaps it's no more than that.

We come very soon to the fallen willow. I glimpse a yellow wagtail beautifully framed in its arch, but we are too intent on getting up speed before having to ship the oars, and aiming at just the right place for me to alert the others, and this time in triumph we shoot straight through, as we soon do with slightly terrifying speed, fearful of damaging the boat, through the shallows below Hannington Bridge.

We slip along among clouds of little gnats and butterflies, still needing to seek the navigable channels among the rushes, but able to pass through much more easily with our extra speed, and with the underwater weed all going our way. The paddle is much more useful too, now we have some way on the boat, and our progress is closer to my jungle fantasies. The river is full of changes. At one moment the bottom is gravelly and the water clear, and at the next the water is clouded with mud and weed. We pass some dead floating fish, giving off what Shakespeare's Trinculo called 'a very ancient and fishlike smell'. We have been told that chub are all succumbing to a disease, but we see plenty of other fish leap, and sometimes huge ones gliding in the shadows. Presumably the numerous fishermen catch something sometimes, though you don't often see it happen.

There is scarcely any wind, and the river reflects the trees and sky and clouds very sharply. Spectacular funguses of both the penny bun and oyster type – sponge or gills – grow on the willows. Brown weed mixed with river mud hangs like shawls, or very ancient cobwebs, over clumps of rushes. Going this way we have more time to notice things, being less intent on the business of merely getting along.

As we go past *The Warm Welcome* once again the schoolgirl in me can't resist, and I sing 'Yah, boo, silly old *Warm Welcome*' and we all blow raspberries, only to see that a man who would be typecast as the unknown Genial Landlord is sitting on a seat at the bottom of his garden. As we realise this, and that he must have heard us, we are so overcome with the weakness of laughing that we can scarcely row ourselves past him. But when we are well past and have wiped our eyes and recovered ourselves, I say:

'Well, he got off lightly. I *could* have been saying, 'May his testicles drop off, may his beer–'' when I freeze at the sight of two shocked ladies sitting on the bank, and my feminist imprecation is never finished. It's as well to remember that banks have hidden ears. I think more than one fisherman must have heard some unusual things during that week.

We're accompanied now by the smell and smoke and rather frightening crackle of stubble burning, which it seems has another year before it is banned. Ecological considerations apart, the sight of the black, acrid fields makes a dismal, ugly end to harvest, after the golden grain and thoughts of fertility. At least the fire can't cross the river.

We meet a lone canoeist going the other way.

'How far is it to Cricklade?'

'About eight miles,' we tell him with the quiet complacency of achievement, and wonder privately if he will make it. He doesn't look to be equipped for overnight.

Somewhere ahead of us among the reeds, an indescribable noise begins, and increases as we approach the source of it. A pair of swans are engaged in the oldest mystery. It does not need the legend of Leda to make us feel we are in the presence of something grand and Olympian. I want to call the sound unearthly, and if that seems an odd word for the act of generation, could it be that that earthliest act that we so cheapen can be one of the bridges between earth and heaven? After all, it has to do with incarnation. Hearing those cries of pleasure-pain we feel awed and intrusive – and deprived. Do human beings ever know real abandonment, or is the restraint bred into us by our inhibition at being overheard too powerful even when we know ourselves alone? But then sparrows only give an extra cheep or two.

Back in Lechlade again we return the paddle – to the bar, since the yard is shut – and they give us back our deposit without question.

'That's unusual,' says an older woman interestedly who is sitting at one of the tables smoking a cigar and doing a crossword with a dictionary. She's referring to our having hired the paddle, and we turn to her instinctively as the matriarch of the place, and on the offchance ask if we can moor for the night at the pub and pitch our tent. And true to the tolerant, easy-going form she has obviously herself created, she says:

'I don't see why not,' and then carefully writes us out a receipt which says:

'Overnight Mooring Row Boat small tent £2 received with thanks.' I have it in front of me, and it seems like a museum piece already.

Emma takes the opportunity to phone her fiancé. Phoebe the extrovert is highly delighted at the prospect of the pub's sociability, and we are all delighted at the womanly welcome from her whom we have privately christened Mrs Big. We put up the tent and make our supper and drink a bottle of pommagne in celebration of our having made it to Cricklade. Then Phoebe takes Emma away to challenge the locals at pool.

As twilight comes I lie in the tent and watch the water for a while, dimpling and dimpling, and put my hand out to feel the rain. And can't. It is very puzzling. Can it be so light, such tiny drops that my skin can't feel what shows so clearly on the river? And then I realise that it isn't rain at all, but the rising of hundreds of tiny fish.

16

At six-thirty it looked like being a fine day, but was still quite cool and breezy. I got up and dressed and went to see if I could find 'Shelley's Walk', which the guidebook said went from the church to the river. It seems that in 1815 Shelley and some friends rowed up from Windsor to Lechlade, and Shelley wrote a poem in the churchyard.

My acquaintance with Shelley is limited. I tried to read him as an undergraduate, but gave up baffled, there seemed nothing I was able – in either sense – to grasp. For my taste there is too little concreteness, too little fact and too much idea. I remember a friend who persevered for longer nevertheless one day saying it was 'great gaseous balls' – which phrase he had found in Shelley's own description, probably of the stuff of the universe, or something equally grand – and then drawing his knees towards his chin in a paroxysm of merriment that was characteristic of him. Alas, as he got older and took himself more seriously he seemed to lose that impish mirth.

But to return to Shelley. I was intrigued at the idea of him having his feet on the ground: the last thing I should have associated him with would have been a footpath. I found that some words from the poem in question had actually been carved on a stone in the churchyard wall:

'Here could I hope that death did hide from human sight sweet secrets'.

This at any rate seemed plain enough: being translated it seemed to mean something like 'if I were able to entertain religious hopes – which I am not – it would be here, in this pretty churchyard (or, presumably, in one like it) on a pleasant summer evening'. (The poem's title is *A Summer Evening Churchyard*.) If you didn't know that Shelley was sent down from Oxford for atheism, and didn't know the rest of the poem, I suppose you might hear in these words something that did not conflict with the pious hopes of the surrounding stones, or even echoed them. Was this the reason that they were cut there, to make Shelley an honourary Anglican? It seems to honour Shelley, to put his words on the wall, to show that Lechlade is proud to have had him visit it. Yet is it not another example of the process of domestication, as has happened with William Morris?

As I walk along 'his' footpath to the river, I ponder over that too. The path has been tarmacked, so that you have no trouble finding it, and you could walk it in winter and be in no danger of mud. Yet some of the pleasure of walking a fieldpath comes from just those elements – its hiddenness, your contact with the earth. A path that is made by the wearing of feet is no more than the other creatures sometimes make, it is a benignly light impression upon nature. To imprison the earth under tarmac and make a mini-road seems ill-judged for any path, but especially for one that is in some sense a memorial of the poet Shelley. If you think of Shelley, the chances are you think of freedom. Or possibly of discarded Harriet, who really does seem to have drowned herself for love of him, in the Serpentine.

Women's feelings must not be allowed to stand in the way of male freedom.

And yet. And yet I enjoyed my walk that morning towards the river, through the open field, and into an arching tunnel of trees where a robin was singing its thin, elegiac, end-of-summer song. There would, we must believe and intend, be other robins, other summers, and though there would never be another Shelley, yet he seemed familiar, and I was glad to have a walk prescribed that made me think of him as having had a body. I was not equipped, either with research and maps or emotionally, for tracking Shelley if it hadn't been obvious. It was very pleasant to be able to walk meditatively, which you can't do if you're hunting for a route. And after all, life does not always have to be a fight in the front line, or a lonely journey in uncharted lands. Sometimes we are grateful for a signpost, or even a metalled road.

I thought about the honour given to poets after they are dead. It's easy to be cynical or angry about that, and living poets often get upset by it, either on their own behalf or on behalf of the poets they feel lacked due recognition while they lived; but perhaps poets are no more and no less deeply heeded when their names are widely known and their works appear on syllabuses than when a few contemporaries were fired by them. The fact that a path has been tamed and some words taken out of context to remind us of Shelley seems more likely to mean that as a nation we honour poetry than that we wish to subvert its threateningly subversive power. The trouble is that the surest way to silence poetry is for the Establishment to honour it. Taking it to heart is always going to be rarer and less quantifiable. Public honour costs very little when the poets are dead or Russian (provided you are not).

It comes to my mind that that potent short story of E.M. Forster's called *The Celestial Omnibus*, has Shelley at the centre, as the prime representative of what Forster thought poetry pointed to. The story tells of how a boy finds an old signpost saying 'To Heaven', and when he asks his parents what it means they tell him it was put there by a disreputable young poet. Even their more cultured friend Mr Bons, who has actually read some Shelley, proves incapable of seeing the reality of what is shadowed in Shelley's poetry. And so Forster metes him out a very violent death. Forster was always tough on the failure to connect. The recent film of *Howard's End* that omits the 'only connect' speech is like *Hamlet* without 'To be or not to be' - which I'm sure has been done too, such, frequently, being the egoism of directors.

But of course, in any case, it is allegory. Mr Bons epitomises the arrogance and complacency that knows it all. He boasts of having 'seven Shelleys' but has no understanding of poetry; and Forster is probably not being vindictive, but simply expressing what he believes happens to such insubstantial furniture, that when it hits the rocks of reality it gets smashed. And he doesn't even tell us the fate reserved for the boy's father, whose mockery was so hurtful to what Jesus called 'one of these little ones'.

I see now what I should have done, if a piece of chalk had been to hand. I should have chalked the words 'to Heaven' on the tarmac path (which one or two showers of rain would have washed away), an ephemeral clue to anyone who could read it. Besides, any footpath can be the narrow way if you can find it.

And come to think of it that is all most of us manage

with the books we write: mere chalk marks for a year or two, and then washed away. But then others will be putting other signs to heaven, perhaps because of signs they themselves have seen and even forgotten, that have led them on nonetheless.

The path comes out by St Johns Lock, where a lone pochard was diving, and a heron stood greyly leaning over the water at an angle as some willows do, and a group of ducks and swans floated placidly. Gulls and terns sat on the river posts, or flew and dived. At this time of the morning the birds had the lock to themselves, and I thought, not for the first time, how foolish it is to turn over in bed and miss the freshness and quiet of two or three hours of light, before many engines are started or many people about. Life seems simpler then, more gracious and full of possibilities.

I walk back by the towpath and fetch up opposite our tent, and call loudly for Emma and Phoebe to get up and fetch me in the boat. This they decline to do, when I eventually manage to wake them up and get them to grasp who and where I am. But they do agree to put the kettle on, so I retrace my steps a short way and cross by Ha'penny Bridge, and come home to a cup of tea and breakfast.

17

'It's curious,' says Phoebe, 'you never know what information is going to come in useful.'

She's referring to the fact that the words '8 till 8' on a shop had happened to catch her eye when we were last in Lechlade, and that this apparently useless piece of information now flashed back onto her mental screen and solved our problem, which was that we wanted to move on, but needed to buy a few things, and were feeling frustrated at the thought of having to wait till nine.

It's said that everything is recorded there, if you could tap into it, from the trauma you have repressed because you don't want to remember it, through your O level chemistry notes which you wanted to remember once and then scrap, only they are still there in 'limbo', to the inconsequential glance like 8 till 8 that you didn't even know you'd taken in. It's difficult not to compare one's brain with a computer these days, and then to get irritated with it for being less efficient. We have such untidy, random databases, and even then there's no infallible procedure to access the stuff we have got.

We generally seem to be far too cluttered in today's world, and it causes a lot of distress; and it can't be the answer to soak up as much knowledge as possible, because clearly whoever invented us had something else in mind

besides a mere mechanical efficiency. The seemingly
disproportionate pleasure we all felt in this seemingly
chance memory of Phoebe's may be a clue to it. Horace
Walpole coined the word 'serendipity' to express it, and a
sure sign of it being somehow involved with our yearning
is that it's a not uncommon boat name.

We moored in mid-afternoon and made tea and Emma
sketched, and Phoebe swam. It was good to watch Phoebe
swimming. I was glad one of us did, and she is a very
strong and competent swimmer, so I wasn't too anxious
about underwater weeds entrapping her, or currents
carrying her off, and could simply enjoy the sight of her
pleasure and competence. The mere thought of going in
myself made my nipples hurt. But thinking about it now, I
wonder if mothers (and wives) need to beware of too much
vicarious living.

We knew that that night we wanted a remote and
beautiful camping place. On other nights we had wanted
lavatories and running water, or other people. Apart from
the night of the man in waterproof trousers we had not yet
camped on our own, and we wanted to experience the
feeling of being alone but peacefully. On the way up we
had noticed long stretches the whole of which looked ideal,
but coming back we seemed harder to please.

To begin with we each had our particular aversion.
Phoebe got jumpy and cross at the idea of mooring near
nettles or mud; Emma was worried about men and swans,
and I had taken against the aspen. I'm obviously not the
only one, because Edward Thomas's poem called *Aspens*
decribes it as a tree 'that ceaselessly, unreasonably grieves,
Or so men think who like a different tree.'

For the most part I'm a devoted admirer of Edward

Thomas's poetry, and I'd always before identified with his faint contempt in those lines for people who didn't like aspens. They wanted their nature bowdlerized, and merely pretty and pleasant. He celebrated nettles too, long before ecology had pointed out how important they are, and raised a better profile for them by making us think of their usefulness to butterflies. But today I was in revolt. I didn't wish to reject anything in nature, I was willing to live and let live, but that didn't mean I didn't want to camp somewhere cheerful. And Thomas is right: it is a question of temperament. I *do* like a different tree – the willow, if I am by the river. It may be the difference between the generally depressive personality like his and the person's who is temporarily grieving. The one will warm to the tree that echoes his world view: the other will look for what brings her back to life. And the willow, as I have said, although associated with grief, has great survival power.

We spot the perfect place ahead, and find of course when we come up to it that it has a launch in it already. We begin to wonder if we haven't passed places we should have settled for. We begin to want supper, and to have some time to sit and enjoy the beautiful place, when we do find it.

When we do find it, it has a cow-pat slap in the middle of it. This in itself was not a disqualification: we can move it, or avoid it. But where are the cows? There are no cows in sight, and what is more there is a wide and deep ditch full of water a few yards in from the bank, which cattle couldn't possibly cross. We gazed about in all directions, and remained baffled. Could it possibly have been put there just to keep us off? It is not that any of us are frightened of cows. It's just that we don't want them nosing about and upsetting the camping gaz, or chewing the tent, or depositing cow-pats on the mooring-ropes, as I had noticed that very morning had happened to one of the launches near Lechlade. I felt quite uncomfortable at the thought of how annoyed those people would be when they woke up and found it there on their nice white rope, and got it on their hands, and then unfastened it to wash it, and the boat floated off with only the women in it, and they were the sort who didn't know how to start the engine, because their job was cooking and cleaning ...

Emma and I set about moving this one, scooping towards each other with the oars. It ought to have been a good idea, an exercise in co-operation and co-ordination, but nonetheless possible. Needless to say, we made slightly more of a mess than had been there before, and dropped the thing, and then had to wash the oars. We ended up piling grass on top of it, and hoping we'd remember to walk round, which shows what an idyllic spot it was, and how little we wanted to row off and look for somewhere else. Later a launch came over, heading happily for this accomodating indentation in the bank, only to find a presumptuous little rowing boat in possession. It was so pleasant that I felt quite sorry for them. They had good taste, like us.

Though unfortunately, we had pot noodles for supper. In a place like that the only proper thing to do would be to sit with our lines in the limpid water until we had some fresh fish to fry, together with a few early mushrooms that were conveniently growing nearby – it was just the right sort of grass. We would follow this with stewed blackberries, and perhaps a bite or two of the goats' cheese we'd bought from a nearby organic farm. The pot noodles had been

Phoebe's idea. She said people were prejudiced about them, and that if Emma and I had never tried them, now was our chance.

A hundred years ago there seems to have been a bit of a craze for the simple life, and for going up the river. Henry Taunt's topographical book about the Thames has an essay at the back recommending it as sovereign against ennui and enthusing about its benefits to mind, body and spirit, and it seems likely that Jerome would have read it, or others like it, and that he endorsed such sentiments. For all his humour and realism, he never undermines those values. He laughs at small follies and vanities, such as fishermen's tall stories about their catch, and he rages, by means of hyperbole, against what he sees as life-denying, like the selfishness of landowners or as symbolized when he represents himself as having astonished the old man who wants him to leave the sunshine and 'Come back and see the skulls!' by quite savagely chiding him away. Jerome's description of their shame-faced retreat back to civilisation in the face of continuous rain in no way detracts from his celebration of holiday, and simplicity, and boating, and outdoors, but merely stops it being over-earnest.

Taunt however was an enthusiast of a different kind, and perhaps a touch solemn about it. He earnestly explains how to equip yourself for the trip, and he commends to your attention the fact that there are now 'so many delicacies in portable form' available on the market. I wonder what he would have thought of pot noodles. Potted meat, or tinned fruit, were exciting then, and fairly unadulterated, and liberating – provided of course that unlike J. and Co. you have remembered the tin-opener. Your late twentieth century pot noodle would seem to be a more advanced form of convenience food, were it not that both designations seem questionable. There was a considerable amount of accurate measurement involved, and the resulting suppers were puzzling. They resembled food, but not in any form, as regards flavour and texture, that we quite recognised: it was like the food might be on another planet.

Phoebe said it was her fault. She said she had added too much water, and let it steep for the wrong amount of time. Personally, I don't believe she was to blame. She's quite a good cook, in a hit-and-miss kind of style, with honest-to-goodness ingredients. But this pot noodle business obviously required the kind of precision more appropriate to the production of some highly unstable substance under laboratory conditions, or to tightrope-walking gourmet cooking for a spoiled and despotic potentate. Emma thought it perhaps an unfair trial, and that we should experiment again under more favourable conditions, or put ourselves in the hands of an experienced pot noodle chef. I thought I wouldn't bother, and would settle another time either for food or for convenience, and not try overweeningly to get them both in one.

We had a curious visitation from a pair of swans. It wasn't at all clear what they wanted. They came over to the boat and hung about hissing and paddling crossly to and fro for a good half hour before they gave up trying to communicate. They had obviously decided we were impenetrably stupid. We were puzzled and apprehensive in equal proportion. Did they want pot noodles; was this their mooring-place; were they simply misanthropic? We were relieved when at last they scornfully turned tail.

Before turning in we played a rather interesting game,

which is trying to decide which three books you would take to a desert island. You rarely get to the stage of everyone's declaring all three, because an intriguing dialogue develops on the way, revealing of personality and priorities. Like most expedition equipment the books need to be able to carry a lot of weight, be strong even though they may be light. They need some of the qualities a boat needs for a voyage of more than an hour or two. Even of the book we'd each brought for this week's trip we demanded more than we should have done where books were freely available.

I'd found the question on a survey form in a public library, and proposed it to the man that I was now trying to get over. I should of course have been seriously worried about his answer, but you ignore warning signs when you're in love. He'd said that he'd definitely take some Dostoievsky, *as he'd need some light relief.* It's just possible he was showing off ('I'm a deep tragic figure') or that it was his idea of a joke ('that's the kind of curmudgeon I am'). At the time I oscillated between these two explanations; but it later occurred to me that perhaps it was sober truth, that his inwardness presented him with as dark a view of life as that came to. Brrr! someone's walked over my grave. Myself, I believe I should have to think seriously about taking *Three Men in a Boat.*

18

At six I crawl damp with sweat from my sleeping bag, intending to sit on the bank and observe the life of the river. Last night I had anticipated doing this in a fresh and receptive mood, but I am full of unquiet thoughts from my dreams, as I leave the tent to sit on the bank. There are huge drops of dew on the tent, and I move the pegs so as to stretch the flysheet further away from the inside. I pull on a sweatshirt over my nightdress and take the ever-useful boat-cushion to sit on. And there is white hair on it, showing up against its dark blue fabric. It gives me a shock, then a small pang of self-pity: I tend to forget I have some of those among the brown. For a split second I thought, What crone has been sleeping in my bed?

It is cool, with a pale sun and a light breeze. I want to let night's shadows go. I want to take reality in. I want to breathe in the fresh life of the outer world and exhale the stale, dark stuff there is inside me. I realise I feel humiliated and unclean to have been hag-rid as I was last night, especially in such a beautiful place. When there are terrible housing estates and tenements where ugly buildings covered in graffiti mock the starving spirit seeking food, and where rage and fear and despair lurk in stinking passageways with bottles in their hands. When there are prisons. Even to say I was hag-rid is an evasion.

Post-Freud we can't get off as simply as that. The stuff is in me.

The sky is pale blue with a few thin veils and striations of white cloud, and the water looks coldly blue, reflecting it. A pheasant called somewhere behind me. Two wood pigeons cross the river. A small fish leaps. My body smells sour from last night's sweated fear, and the evil psychic odour of the dream seems to cling to my spirit in the same way.

There was art, that was it, an exhibition of the art produced in a place where you were watched all the time. It was *clean* art, it seemed very wholesome. It had a kind of rugged, peasant innocence and simplicity. It was very *good*, morally speaking, that is, if you take 'good' as in 'what a good little girl' rather than as in 'good Hamlet, cast thy nighted colour off'... Ah, the twist of the knife again, never even a clean wound: for the queen is pleading with Hamlet to be good, to be kind, not to punish her with his withdrawal into the dark – and *she* was *guilty!* Am I guilty, more than anyone else? But the dream ...

There is tremendous splashing in the reeds a few yards up. Was it sex or a fight or merely a waterfowl enjoying the sensation of the drops being showered and getting right up under its wings? The fact that there is no other sound, no squawk or hiss, and it subsides quite quickly, suggests the last is the most likely. I would be the better if I did the same myself. Inwardly too. And there's a paradox: my body shivers and relucts at the thought of it, and I draw my knees up closer; but it's my spirit that more deeply dreads those icy drenches of reality, and seems to hug the fetid darkness that has been swaddling it.

But the dream: the society that seemed so faultless, so

perfectly regulated, and yet my intuition telling me there was a price, knowing that it was kept controlled by some invincible tyrant. Trying to teach my children how to keep their integrity in this deceptively clean place. And then the confrontation. Then the smiling villain speaks to me in a quiet purr at this latest art exhibition which seems to prove what a beautiful world his is. His eyes are cold blue as the river looks this morning. He doesn't need to say much. Instead he points. In the corner of the room, in an alcove, is an operating table, and surgical instruments. 'You see,' he says, still very quiet but at least paying my calibre the compliment of no longer smiling. And I see that if ever I pluck up the courage to show people how their free will has been taken or given away, I risk mine being taken away permanently and physically.

Alright, I see. The tyrant is in me, repressing the self that says repression is not the way to make a beautiful person or to make good art. The tyrant has got my number, and threatens more openly now he knows that I have got his. Good and evil, real and ideal, handy dandy, which is which. A heron flying slowly over quite high up and catching the sunlight is such a relief. Archaic, somehow, and unhurried, and restfully *other*, not fashioned by my own fearful brain.

Behind me cattle are calling, though it's still not clear how they can have crossed the ditch. Further off there are swirls of mist being blown along the water. The current and the breeze are going the same way and there are ripples. The two wood pigeons are fooling heavily around in a hawthorn and making some leaves fall off. It is lovely to thrash around with the one you love until the duvet falls off. Does this coupling world ever hurt less to the ones no longer loved?

A soft *proop!* from the reeds every so often, but otherwise the river is empty. The sun is a little higher now and has begun to warm me. Then a pair of kingfishers, flying low and fast upstream, veer off to one side with a sun-touched flash of their orange fronts, then veer again to blue.

And now the stage of the river starts to fill up again, after this brief opening scene between the stars. First a crow crosses over. Then martins fly in from the wings and make their high calls as they swoop. One of the wood pigeons tumbles out of bed and goes off to make the tea. A single wader goes past upstream as if it knows where it's going, and a couple of duck fly across from bank to bank. Some way upstream I can see a lone coot feeding near the reeds, and in the nearer clump of reeds there is continual chatter from the sedge-warblers. The pigeons' domestic saga continues. One of them flies across and back, and they are in and out of the may tree and onto the ground, as though they were getting breakfast. A small contingent of blackheaded gulls go upstream purposefully. How lovely to know where you're going as clearly as that!

I had woken in the night and seen strange flashes of light through the fabric of the tent. I'd thought at first that someone was coming with a big torch and I lay there locked in fear. Then it continued and got nearer and I realised the flashes were too big for a torch – and why should it flash in any case? Then I thought it was summer lightning, but I didn't dare look out, in case it struck me. There was no thunder, no relief of rain. It also seemed possible when I thought about it later that it had been a plane, though if so it was curiously bright. Eventually I went to sleep again, and as I now recall, also dreamt that my father *was telling me what to do*, though I can't recall his ever doing so, and my feeling of utter rage.

A chunk of reed-bed floats by, going slowly, like a hearse. I wonder who can have torn it off and why. The water is making a pleasant slopping noise against the side of the boat. The sedge-warblers are still conversing, now from within and now from in front of the reed curtain. They have probably been up since four.

I get some human breakfast ready and open the curtain of the tent, and wake the girls from their less appalling dreams. An hour by the river in silence is not a bad morning draught for emotional hangover; take it followed by friendly talk and tea, if possible.

19

A single tern dived, as we untied and pushed off. They are shaped so perfectly as tools for the purpose, the flat head, and the angled wings which are suddenly and swiftly folded so that the streamlined body can drop like an arrow. They are quite differently made from the looser, rounder-winged, scavenging gulls with which they often mingle, but which do not dive. The combination of strength and grace, the control of the flight and then the abandonment to the fall give me great delight to watch. I had forgotten or never noticed that terns came to inland water and their company that week added an unforeseen pleasure.

And then an unfamiliar bird goes past; we can't make it fit with anything we expect to see, and we come to the conclusion that it is a cormorant. It seems to be being bowled along by the current, but then it takes off and flies quite strongly.

Each species has its unique and characteristic qualities, without which the world would be the poorer. It is something that we need a word for. Bird-watchers talk about the 'jizz', that something that makes a thing itself and no other, but it's an awkward word without the resonance of an etymology. Hopkins called it 'inscape', but somehow literary critics have hijacked the word. They write several paragraphs of complex prose purporting to elucidate it, and only succeed in persuading us we haven't really understood. Which is a pity, for it is a vital notion, literally vital, having to do with life enfleshed in a particular way.

Emma wiped her nose on her skirt.

'I don't think it makes much difference at this stage,' she said when we remonstrated, and we all laughed. We were all feeling rather pleasantly dirty, an outdoor, summer sort of dirtiness that is quite different from an indoor, winter sort. It was not irksome to us because we did not need to feel constrained. It seemed a more natural state of life than the biologically washed and ironed and deodorised life of jobs and offices and indoors. Not that clean clothes are not a pleasure, and hot baths. But after a day or two of hankering for them the habit loses its hold and you seem to enter a different state of being, becoming more relaxed and happy in your skin. As we rowed easily along, still enjoying the current in our favour of course, we realised how much fitter we felt in every way – in ways that mere regimens of exercises could never produce. We were experiencing ease. We laughed a lot at nothing much, and the world, even to me, looked kinder than it had a week ago.

The sun was out again too, after having been so helpfully veiled for the greater part of our strenuous days. And the black dog doesn't flourish in the sun; it is too flat a contradiction of his view of life.

We rowed gently along looking out for blackberries, which we remembered noticing in Shifford Cut on the way up. When packing my pruning instinct sometimes goes too far, and I'd both left my cheque book at home and underestimated the cash.

I'd also forgotten to pack any tampons. There's a definite Sod's Law factor about that, very similar to the one that governs umbrellas. In fact, it may even be the case that anxiety at being unprovided with them increases the likelihood of their being required. Anyhow we calculated that if tampons were included when we passed the shop we'd have about five pence left, and no pudding for tonight. Besides which, our artificially straitened circumstances, the seeming necessity, added spice to our already keen living-off-the-land instinct.

This instinct is often especially strong in childhood. I know of two girls of nine who 'ran away' from home and were discovered by the river plaiting willow sticks together, having decided to live by making baskets. But it often persists into adult life. A friend of mine is almost impossible to go walking with on account of it – if you wish to have a conversation that is, and walk relatively unburdened. She is for ever catching sight of hazel nuts in awkward places, or stopping to quarter a field for mushrooms, or borrowing your belt to make an ingenious strap-carrier for irresistible bits of kindling wood.

The three of us were all quite well-endowed with it, and besides, the challenge of blackberrying from the boat was novel. It proved quite exciting. Phoebe was rowing, and as soon as we saw some we urged her to 'Stop!' and 'Back a bit, no, that way' and so on, which commands cannot very easily be complied with in a rowing boat, especially when it is going with the current. She did her best, and I leaned out keenly from the stern as soon as we were almost near enough and almost fell in. Once you are near enough to touch the bank of course it is impossible to row any more, so we drifted off again and came in at a different angle.

This time the boat headed fast and straight for the bank and plunged itself deep into the bramble bush, and I had to throw myself backwards into the boat to avoid being torn to pieces, and then disengage one of the oars and push us off with it.

Next Phoebe swung the nose of the boat in and it was Emma's turn. She was at a pitch of eager impatience by this time and she brought all her faculties to bear on the job. She actually got a berry in each hand before we drifted past. Then Phoebe began to develop the necessary skill, and found some way of going parallel with the bank. The trouble was we still had to be about a yard out from it, and Emma and I would both lean out at the same time, and the boat would be at forty-five degrees and we would glare at each other and tell each other to 'Watch out!' until we felt quite ill-tempered. I said we must make it a rule not to stand up, and we agreed it was a good idea.

But Emma was quite unable to keep to it. The sight of large clutches of gleaming blackberries just out of her reach from a sitting position was too much for her, and picking deftly and intently she'd rise up by degrees like something that's been stuck down with too light a glue and gradually works itself free. Then Phoebe who'd been rather selflessly rowing all this while, and hadn't had a chance to pick at all, got mad at our repeated, and contradictory orders, and at the difficulty of the thing, and said she didn't like us shouting 'Ouch, ouch, bugger!' in cross voices when we got scratched, as though it was her fault. So I did my best to hold the boat close by holding on to a branch while she had a go.

I have a method I rather pride myself on, of picking several berries into one hand. It is fast, and quite skillful, but it does mean that quite a lot of juice gets on to me. And besides that, when you are trying to pick from a moving target you tend to snatch rather than pick gently. At the end of half an hour we had about half a pound of berries and we looked, with 'our purpled hands' like the conspirators in *Julius Caesar*, and quite expected Mark Anthony to show up and start making speeches and shaking hands with us.

On the upstream journey we had noticed from time to time some powdery blue berries which were unfamiliar to us. Phoebe had tried in vain to find them in the flower book. With their matt appearance they were not unlike blue raspberries. They had an edible look, and I think we half-hoped they might turn out to be something like Water Skyberries, otherwise known as Boatman's Breakfast, a water-loving plant, localised and highly prized for its delicious fruit. We'd already passed up a wonderful ruby red desert gooseberry, which some bird must long ago have sown on the bank, just because it looked so much like something from *Goblin Market*, too good to be true; and I became pusillanimous and decided it *wasn't* true, and might be something poisonous. We pulled over to the Skyberries and found that they were blackberries in a coating of grey mould. Weeks later, to my great annoyance, I came across them in a book. I am almost certain they must have been *dewberries*, which *are* edible and have a much more properly poetic name.

Shifford Lock was mentioned in our guide, which was this year's, as having a Ladies, but the lock-keeper shook his head.

'No,' he said, 'not any more. The Residents pulled it down.' We were on another planet again. We felt like travellers in a science fiction story who fetch up on a planet where there's a war on, or a totalitarian government and an underground movement, and have to tread warily till they find out who is fighting who and why. On the face of it a toilet didn't seem important strategically. But perhaps the Residents were men terrified of women's dominance, like that *Times* columnist of a hundred years ago that Jerome had quoted, and like, come to think of it, most of the men we knew. Presumably their plan was to reduce us to squatting behind bushes and then go aha! and make us wet our knickers and sting our bums on the stinging nettles and then have to moor again and find another bush further off. On the other hand, all that would be needed to have a jolly joke like that would be an 'Out of Order' notice.

Pulling down sounded quite a laborious business, one that involved a sterner principle than mere common or garden misogyny. We pictured them standing around with gloves on, doing it brick by brick, the little children watching in awed silence, aware that they were part of history.

'You will be able to tell *your* children how you actually witnessed the destruction of one of the thrones of public convenience', they would say to them. 'You must remember it, and tell them how there once were places that were not Privatised, places where Anybody could go, sometimes even without paying.'

It seems in any case a curiously perverse state of affairs when the Residents of a lock cottage are not the lock-keeper and family, who must then have to live somewhere else, and the Residents, when not engaged in Pulling Down ceremonies, must have to go somewhere else to work. The National Rivers Authority, like Shakespeare's Bassanio, give out 'rare new liveries' but wherever we went their employees up and down the river seemed less cheerful than his were, and often seemed to be engaged in long querulous conversations about the set-up, involving a good deal of '...it just doesn't make sense' and 'I can't see how they think ...'.

There is much to be inferred from titles. The Thames Conservancy suggests the love and knowledge of a particular river, and caring for it. The word Authority, besides being a hubristic misnomer – since clearly Mother Nature, if not indeed the Author and Giver of all good things, is being overlooked – implies power rather than stewardship. And ever since British Rail started calling us customers instead of passengers the service has got worse and worse.

The lock-keeper said that as the Residents were out, Phoebe could slip round the back and use the loo he was allowed to use. It turned out to be a pretty standard model, suggesting they weren't aliens at all, but people with bums and digestive organs etc. pretty much like ours, if not identical.

We stopped for coffee at The Maybush, a treat included in our budget, and sat in the garden and looked at the bridge. While we sat drinking our coffee and admiring the view, and Emma was drawing it, a man came and gave us a lecture on it. He had obviously done it before. His manner was curious. He talked rapidly and monotonously, and clearly conversation was not his purpose, because he seemed put out by our questions or interjections. I mention a single fact – gleaned from our guidebook – and he is jealous and suspicious – Where did I get that from? In Jerome's day you might have assumed he wanted money, but today we can only suppose that the sight of three women obviously ignorant and in need of information was too much for him. We thanked him politely, and he went off none the wiser, obviously feeling that he had discharged a duty.

Old New Bridge, one of the oldest on the river, is pleasant to the eye, as most building is that has endured for several centuries. It is a patchwork of great grey and yellow stones six arches wide of immense solidity, but so clearly part of a slower age that to see cars and lorries crossing it creates a small shock of incongruity. There are wooden fenders in front of the piers, presumably to prevent a flimsy, shiny, ill-steered launch from hurting itself on the nasty stone. These structures are made of wood weathered to the same grey as the stone, and even more curiously some lengths of new wood, perhaps let in where the old ones did fall foul of one of the launches, are just the same yellow as the yellow stones in the bridge. But then nature tends to harmonise, and wood and stone are natural materials, friendly to eye and hand. There are streaks of brown in a grey squirrel's tail that match autumn leaves and nuts. I once observed that the light oak screen in Inglesham Church, that William Morris restored to its mediaeval state, is the colour of the little beaches of river sand not half a mile off. And that is not an irrelevant coincidence, for we carry colours in our inner eye, and the psyche lives on such things. It cannot but minister to our inner harmony that inside a beautiful riverside church we receive an echo of the river and vice versa, and we do whether our conscious mind has registered it or not.

20

The poet Edward Thomas identified two opposing tendencies within us – that which wanders over the earth in search, and that which wants to settle and build a home. I imagine that these two needs are there in us all, but mixed in different proportions, and urgent perhaps at different times in our lives. Each might label the other 'escapist', but it might be wiser to call each other friend, or sister or brother. There are times when our idylls fall apart, and we can sometimes try and try again to rebuild them; or we can enter a more exploratory state, and be open as new ideas present themselves. Or we may wander for years, never certain that here is the place to dig in, and hang up our boots, until finally somewhere – and perhaps someone – says 'This is it'. These are partly metaphors, of course; and besides, it is never clear-cut. We may be the settler in one aspect of our lives while being at the same time the wanderer in another. In fact, that is usually the case if we want to grow, for rootless plants can no more grow than fossils can breathe again.

The names people give their boats have more pathos about them even than those they give their houses. A house is more earnest and quotidian than a boat. For a boat we can give reign to our fantasy, and the name is sometimes a window into the heart, a registering of a central longing or preoccupation. *Day Dreams* was the name of one launch that overtook us from time to time, which, being translated, really only means boat, for the name encapsulates all the functions of a pleasure craft. You are free for the time being from the importunities of the workaday world, whether actual, from outside, or the invisible and inner 'oughts' which tell you, even if not actually at work, that you should pay the bills or paint the fence or ask the neighbours in. You are free for a while to dream, but it is a waking dream, one you have made actual, even if only in a weekend and temporary way.

You get a few names from *The Wind in the Willows* – Toad, Rat, Badger, Pan – but many more, oddly it might seem, from Tolkien. Why, especially when hobbits were notoriously water-shy, should there be this association of Middle-Earth with boats? I think the answer is in the alternative and greener world that makes the measure of value in the books. Some would call it escapist, but Tolkien himself importantly distinguished between the escape of the prisoner and the flight of the deserter, a distinction that is often lost sight of in argument. It would be useful if the word 'escapist' could be reclaimed from its derogatory use.

On a holiday, or on a journey, both of which we were then, you are favoured with glimpses of other people's dreams and diggings in. We pass a boathouse with a name up – Eden End. Presumably the name is formed on the analogy of other substantial places. I think of Bag End and Howard's End, in literature. The 'End' must imply a detatched house in some ground, and 'Eden' expresses how much whoever gave it the name appreciated the rural spot. My persistent fantasy in adolescence involved a house not unlike this with a garden that came down to the river's edge, where a boat was moored, so I can enter into some of the feeling. But the innocent hubris, if I can so describe it, of using the name of Eden seems almost to equal that of the two inhabitants of the original place before they ate the apple. Isn't it asking for trouble?

But then trouble has come, of course, already. Eden ended, Eden was out as a place where human beings could be, even before a second generation. And where Eden ends, there the world begins. Eden is not an option, the alternatives are only what we can manage in the postlapsarian world. Looked at like that, the name seems to suggest the collapse of an idyll, though of course no-one would commemorate that in a name. But it can be read in a purposeful, realistic way: recognising that Eden is over, and that life is to be begun at precisely that point and in that realisation and acceptance of necessity, seems a necessary solid foundation, even if visions remain to inspire us and help us build. Someone there had trained a rose to ramble up a willow, and it has a delicate, unkempt beauty. In Eden no doubt such beauties were more abundant and readily compassed, without being scratched, or breaking the spade, or putting out your back, or having to buy the rose from a catalogue. But they could not be more beautiful. A dark green damsel fly lights for a minute or so on Emma's bare arm as she rows.

The place has been named, of course, after the planet. The world is Eden End, and everything we do or say is either part of the continuing demolition job, or else it is part of making the world more lovely. The name of Eden names our deepest longings. It speaks of loss even without the addition of End. Eden has ended, is always ending, but we can sow a seed or two, or plant a tree, or prune a tree, or smell the flowers and let them sweeten us, or praise the garden's labourers in a poem.

Up and down the river this week we have read the boat names – jokes both public and private, conundrums, pretensions, affections, affectations, dreams. But particularly dreams. On your white launch, with your suntan and sunglasses, a bottle of booze and a couple of glasses and a woman, you can play that you are the king of the castle. How you bear down on things, with your peaked cap and your lordly torso! Or on your green canal boat, with your ample breasts and your old flowered skirt and straw hat, a teapot and a couple of cups and a man, you can play you are queen of the garden. How you will heal things and make soup for everyone, with your ladle and herbs in tubs on the roof! And you name the boat to emphasise these points.

Oh, the simplicity of ducks, of those half dozen, sleeping so quietly with their heads turned onto their backs! They seemed to us at the time to be all females, and back at home I looked in a book to find out where the males all went at the latter end of summer. And it seems it is a matter of seasonal plumage: the males are in 'eclipse', so the sexes look alike. The restfulness of sleep-time in the sun in the unsexual phase communicates itself by means of calm vibrations to the world around.

But now a little wind gets up and blows against us, and the sun is hidden and we go past the dreary derelict pub at Bablockhythe, where for over ten centuries there was a ferry, but not any more, and along from where at present there is not even a pub any more, there is a mile of caravans where, the notice says, you are not to play ball or ride a bike. These were two prohibitions new to us: no mooring, and no fishing we were used to.

A curious set of commandments could be put together from all the notices you see about the place: No waiting, No stopping, No ice creams in here, No-one without shoes, No men without ties, No talking, No transistors, No walking on the grass, No picking flowers ... No wonder Jesus thought we'd got the wrong approach. Those of these Thou Shalt Nots which are not mere tyranny Love would never offend against. But then you can't put up notices saying LOVE, it seems too obvious to be necessary and at the same time too hard to see how to do it. How, for example, can you love a man who doesn't want to play ball?

It is yet another manifestation of the side of our nature that makes the pylons and the mink coats and the bomber planes and the barbed wire. The negative makes ugly marks on the world whereas love on the whole is less visible in itself, since it wants you to enjoy the lovely world. The signs saying PUBLIC FOOTPATH are an exception, and all possessiveness or wanton destructiveness can do is to pull them down, like they did the loo. And they frequently do. But in any case the footpath system would not be needed by love. And in Sweden, which is not Eden, people even have the right to roam wherever – within reason – they like, and it seems to work.

You cannot even roam up the Thames without a licence. We were asked for ours in a couple of locks, and the first time we felt like Beatrix Potter's Pigling Bland when he searched in all his pockets and couldn't find it. Were they going to turn us back, or make us take the boat out of the water there and then? We knew the boat was licensed for

the Thames, but we didn't know where or whether this fact
was displayed. Eventually we found it on the back of the
seat, and changed from outlaws and hippies to smug law-
abiding citizens in an instant. We row peacefully on 'down
the stripling Thames to Bablockhythe'.

Bablockhythe is no place to think about Matthew Arnold
any more: it is a place to row past as quick as you can and
forget about. In fact all the Matthew Arnold places have
lost the rural freshness that they must have had in the
Scholar Gipsy's day. They are built on and polluted by
traffic noise and have the stale and fly-blown air of land
where too many people from a town are trying to relax and
make believe that they are in the country. But none is
sadder than this bit of river with its poetic place-name,
made doubly poetic by Arnold's famous line. Even our
sober and mainly factual, mainly affirmative guidebook
called it 'unwelcoming'.

And yet, since I have been thinking about both waking
and sleeping dreams, I cannot help but think of *Dover
Beach*:

> Ah, love, let us be true
> To one another! for the world, which seems
> To lie before us like a land of dreams,
> So various, so beautiful, so new,
> Hath really neither joy, nor love, nor light,
> Nor certitude, nor peace, nor help for pain...

Arnold saw the world in this light, or rather in this shadow,
when he reflected on the widespread loss of religious faith.
I think he meant something far deeper by this than people
feeling unable to accept a string of preposterous articles of
belief. He meant that in the chill wind of materialism the

world was no longer a holy place, and he realised with pain what this would mean in terms of the breakdown of community and the sense of the world as commodity rather than as gift. Perhaps it was too much to ask of a single love relationship that it should keep him warm in this dark mood. Perhaps he was wiser when he wrote in *Self-Dependence* that he should learn from nature how to be himself, noting how 'with joy the stars perform their shining':

> For alone they live, nor pine with noting
> All the fever of some differing soul.

21

We glimpse the sleek head of a swimming mink, having thought for a glorious second or two that it was an otter, before we fetch up once again at Eynsham Lock, feeling like old hands. We moor and pitch the tent and Emma and Phoebe go off to post some cards, and I go and hang around at the lock and help with the gates. When we went through the locks in the boat we usually stayed in it. It's not so easy to get in and out of it as it is to step on and off a launch or a narrowboat, and we want to be ready to go and not hold people up. But still I have a guilty feeling we haven't been pulling our weight. And in any case I would like the lock-keeper to talk aboout river matters. At the end of a week I am just beginning to have an inkling of my ignorance.

But he wants to talk about John McCarthy, who has just been released from prison. Away from the radio and newspapers, we haven't heard about it, and this word of mouth was our news, as it always would have been once. Telling and hearing a piece of joyful news makes a pleasant exchange. I am glad to have heard it from another human being, and he is glad to tell someone new what the rest of the world has known for twenty-four hours.

This news coming near the end of our trip brings us back to the world we have left behind. The world we have

stepped away from for a space is one where innocent
people can be imprisoned against their will, where
sometimes people cannot, for all kinds of reasons, and even
with a licence, have the simple pleasure of taking a boat up
the Thames and sleeping in the open air, or even of seeing
the sun and stars.

'Gone to the pub, your daughters, have they?' asks the
lock-keeper.

'No,' I say, 'not this time. We've run out of money.'

Whereupon he becomes really concerned, says we
needn't have paid for our mooring, and even offers to lend
us some.

'Are you alright for supper?' he later wants to know. For
a moment it seems as though we are in the world of *News
from Nowhere* – although of course there they don't use
money at all – but where everyone is truly neighbourly.
We thank him warmly and I wonder anxiously if I would
have done the same in his place, or felt the same interest in
a stranger's welfare.

Next morning we pack the tent up and strike camp for
the last time. We can do it in a very few minutes now,
without much need for words. Since that first night in this
same place, when we were ill-equipped and unpractised,
we have acquired some skill and competence. It is one of
the several reasons we are more relaxed now. We feel
capable as well as blessed.

It is beginning to be another hot day, but we have plenty
of time to be back in Oxford by mid-day when our hire
time runs out, and we all enjoy the wide, quiet, empty
river, shared with a grebe that dives and comes up with a
silver fish in its mouth, the sense of leisure and of sun-
warmed peace. Wytham Woods are piled handsomely up

across the meadows on one bank and timeless-looking
Oxfordshire villages with their spires and grey stone
cottages can be glimpsed across the width of their harvest
fields on the other. We row along peacefully and not too
fast.

And then out of the blue:

''F you do that you'll get muscles like an elephant's
knee-caps', a man says viciously to Emma, who is rowing,
as he passes us noisily in a small powered boat. Emma says
nothing. Being Engaged, she is in a state in which it is
possible to see oneself as having solved a problem
personally, and to believe that the odd barbarian does not
disclose an endemic problem. Phoebe's face darkens, but
she too doesn't want to think about it. The men she knows
are more enlightened ... aren't they? She brushes the
thought impatiently away, as she would a horsefly.

I brood, of course. What is the story behind a remark
like that? The major substance of it is insult, mixed with
threat and warning. It is not the standard badinage of the
river, though that often has more than a hint of sexism in it.
The tone was savage. Emma is young and beautiful, and
the implication was that if she takes healthy exercise her
body will become less attractive to men. He took on
himself to be spokesman for his sex, and the anger in his
tone showed he thought he was being deprived of a right.
He must also have reckoned that he had the right to issue
such a warning, uninvited, to a perfect stranger. It
announced his lust of course, which many women consider
to be out of order even when couched as simple
admiration.

But of course it is not admiration that lies behind a
remark like that, but deep-seated fear and mysogyny. If

women get strong, in muscle or even more to the point in independence, they might start thinking men were overrated. That they didn't need men to row the boat.

I feel depressed as you do when you think there's been progress and are shocked to encounter regression. When I was a student I used to visit a fellow-student who later became my husband. The common room of his college had a book where remarks and requests were jotted, and where one day was written:

'Why doesn't Taplin's girlfriend shave her legs?'

As it happens my legs were not in those far-off days making a feminist stand, but betrayed a mere lack of self-consciousness. It hadn't occurred to me to think about them. So my reaction then was to be mortified, to feel that I'd let the aforesaid Taplin down.

The college in question now takes women students, and Phoebe and Emma, who had both been students until recently, assured me that such a remark would be outlawed in such circles for the possessive designation of so-and-so's girlfriend, just as much as for its question. I hope so. But my fear is that though what it's politically correct to say may alter (in mixed company at any rate) the naked chauvinist feelings may be merely covered up. Men can delude themselves as well as deceiving us.

It would be so good to share the boat of life with a man who liked to take turns at the oars. Rowing and being rowed are both so enjoyable; to deprive ourselves of either seems unbalanced. I have not managed it ever, and my generation has a disastrous record of marriages breaking down or lasting but on a lopsided basis. And though I am still too English to howl abandonedly, I have wanted to say plainly: *It hurts, it bloody hurts, what men have done to us.*

It would be so good to think that things might be different for Phoebe and Emma. The enjoyment of our week together has had so much to do with equality and co-operation. Women are in the same boat, there's no doubt about that. Which is why unsisterliness is even more horrible than male chauvinism, though it's probably a side effect of it.

Do-as-you-would-be-done-by is at least of some use to us there. But how good it would be if we could recognise that we are *all* in the same boat, women and men alike, all fearful, all needing love, all sharing the same planet, because we shan't stop hurting each other and the earth till we do.

We are back at Folly Bridge. And this time stepping onto the jetty seems the folly, not setting out. While we were on the river we became increasingly merry and free. The Oxford traffic and Saturday crowds are horrible. Christ Church Meadow is a Babel of tourists. The heat which had been pleasant on the water is savage on the man-made roads and pavements. I make a noise and fumes with my car engine. A policeman tells me off for waiting on the bridge.

But I fancy that Emma's boyfriend looks at her newly glowing aura with newly kindled pleasure, and Phoebe looks fit and ready to face her students, and I know the week has brought me some new health and peace. I can't quite sing with Ariel that I shall always live merrily now that my summer is over, but I believe I have discovered some ways to deal with the black dog. I shan't always be able to manage it; but I know he cringes away from air and sunlight, when you stand your ground, when you love created things, when you make affirmations, and would vanish altogether if you could let him go.

Other titles in the Travellers' Tales series:

Journey Along the Andes
From Bolivia, through Peru and Ecuador, to Columbia
Christopher Portway
ISBN 1 874687 12 9 £5.95

The Drive-thru Museum
A journey across the everyday USA
Andy Soutter
ISBN 1 874687 09 9 £4.95

Indian Odyssey
Around the subcontinent by public transport
Christopher Portway
ISBN 1 874687 14 5 £5.95

By Bicycle in Ireland
A personal guide to Irish landscapes
Martin Ryle
ISBN 0 245 54666 9 £4.95

A Gringo's Journey
A bicycle journey from North America to Southern Chile
Cris Osborn
ISBN 0 245 55066 6 £4.95

Kevin and I in India
Travels around the subcontinent
Frank Kusy
ISBN 0 245 54417 8 £4.95

Back to Mandalay
An inside view of Burma
Gerry Abbott
ISBN 0 245 60135 X £5.95

Lemurs of the Lost World
Exploring the forests and Crocodile Caves of Madagascar
Jane Wilson
ISBN 0 245 60045 0 £5.95

The Islands in Between
Travels in Indonesia
Annabel Sutton
ISBN 0 245 54829 7 £5.95

Distant Shores
By traditional canoe from Asia to Madagascar
Sally Crook
ISBN 0 245 60044 2 £5.95

A Winter in Tibet
Letters from Lhasa
Charles and Jill Hadfield
ISBN 0 245 54773 8 £5.95

Other travel titles from Impact Books/Olive Press:

Bicycle Breaks
Between London and the sea
Martin Ryle
ISBN 0 245 06332 8 £5.95

Watching the Dragon
Letters form China
Charles and Jill Hadfield
ISBN 0 245 54390 2 £8.95

Sea and Sardinia
D.H. Lawrence
ISBN 0 946889 20 1 £6.95

Etruscan Places
D.H. Lawrence
ISBN 0 946889 13 9 £6.95

The Other Italy
David Price
ISBN 0 946889 01 5 £3.50

Travels in Japan
David Price
ISBN 0 946889 14 7 £6.95

152

A Better Class of Blond
A California diary
ISBN 0 946889 04 X £4.50

The Scent of India
Pier Paolo Pasolini
ISBN 0 946889 02 3 £4.95

Assignments in Africa
Per Wästberg
ISBN 0 946889 11 2 £5.95